THE WORLD'S BEST DAD

DURING & AFTER DIVORCE

FAMILIUS

Published by Familius LLC, www.familius.com
1254 Commerce Way, Sanger, CA 93657

Familius books are available at special discounts for bulk purchases,
whether for sales promotions or for family or corporate use.
For more information, contact Familius Sales
at 559-876-2170 or email orders@familius.com.

Library of Congress Control Number: 2020941606

Print ISBN 9781641702683
Ebook ISBN 9781641703628

Printed in the United States of America

Edited by Lindsay Sandberg and Alison Strobel
Cover and book design by Mara Harris

10 9 8 7 6 5 4 3 2 1
First Edition

THE WORLD'S BEST DAD
AFTER DIVORCE

A GUIDE TO CO-PARENTING
FOR DIVORCED DADS

PAUL MANDELSTEIN

"Whether he knows it or not, and no matter what his position in society, the father is the initiating priest through whom the young being passes into the larger world."
—Joseph Campbell

CONTENTS

INTRODUCTION

*"When one door closes, another door opens; but we so often look
so long and regretfully upon the closed door, that we do not see
the ones which open of us."*
—*Alexander Graham Bell*

Tim and Gina met while on vacation in Southern California. Tim had just gotten a dream promotion at his first serious job. Now manager of the marketing department at Quantum, he was riding high and confident of his future. Gina, however, was just coming out of a painful breakup with the young man she'd been dating for two years.

Gina certainly wasn't looking for a new relationship. But that was before she met Tim. She welcomed Tim's company, but made it clear that she was only interested in having someone to pal around with. Tim said okay, though he was absolutely certain he'd found the love of his life. He'd take his time, give her whatever space she needed. He believed that if he was patient and played his cards right, everything would work out. Tim's patient attention was exactly what Gina needed to help her through this difficult time.

The long and short of it is that after several months of telephone conversations across the miles—she in Tucson, he in Seattle—they agreed to meet in San Francisco over Labor Day weekend. Gina was ready to give love another chance.

The weekend in San Francisco couldn't have been more perfect. Six months later, they were making wedding plans. Gina chose a traditional church wedding, which was fine with Tim as long as they could have a large reception at a place near the ocean, with all their friends celebrating with them. This was one marriage, they told their friends, that would last forever.

It in fact lasted for nine and a half years, long enough for Alexia and Ben to be born. Neither Gina nor Tim could remember when the arguments actually started. They were over small things at first, but soon, even the small disagreements were turning into major fights. They kissed and made up time after time. It seemed that no matter what one of them suggested to the other, it was steel on flint. Sparks flew, whether the discussion was what to fix for dinner, what to plant in the garden, where to spend their vacation, or issues involving the kids. The loving intimacy they'd once shared eroded with each argument. Finally, they were sleeping in different rooms, and Tim sought every opportunity for out of town business trips. Gina noticed she was more relaxed when Tim was out of town, and she avoided intimate contact when he was home.

Tim and Gina both felt very alone in their marriage, depressed, and anxious by the loss of support they'd once shared with each other. It was nearly impossible for either of them to accept the fact that something that started so beautifully had come to this.

The children, now five and seven, were beginning to show the signs of the constant tension between their parents. In family counseling, Gina and Tim struggled through the challenges of their own conflicts. In the beginning, they both made a pledge to stay together and resolve their differences. Somehow, they'd make the marriage work. Above all, they both understood the negative impact their separation would have on the kids, and they wanted to avoid this at all costs—well, *nearly* all costs.

It all came to a head at Alexia's soccer game, when Tim and Gina started arguing in front of the kids and other parents. Deeply humiliated by their own behavior and aware of how they'd also humiliated their own children, they apologized to the people around them and made their way home. Although they were still furious with each other, that evening, they made a pact to never again air their conflicts in public. And they would try their best to not argue in front of the kids.

Their conflicts persisted in spite of all their efforts, and the tension continued to impact Alexia and Ben. At last, after much soul-searching and tears, Tim and Gina looked at each other across their therapist's office one February morning and made the decision to end their marriage. It was the first thing they'd agreed on in months. They also made a pledge, suggested by their counselor, to make the break with a specific goal in mind—to do everything in their power to treat one another with respect and dignity. With two beautiful children, they had much to be grateful for. The marriage had blessed them in this way, regardless of the fact that they could no longer live together. The therapist assured them that she would be available to help them through the separation, guiding them through what she called "collaborative divorce."

HONORING THE BONDS
OF OUR CHILDREN

Like Tim and Gina, most of us enter into marriage with the firm belief that our union with last forever. But life is rarely that simple. If you are now facing the prospect of divorce, have already taken the first step in that direction, or are maybe only beginning to contemplate its inevitability, you already know the wildly vacillating complex of feelings that have led up to this point.

Try as we might, it is impossible to know, with absolute certainty, that separating from your partner is the right way to go. What you do know is that you are in pain and your partner is in pain and that your children are in pain. At the very least, your kids may be showing the stresses of your struggle through uncharacteristically aggressive behavior, by having trouble with school work, or by any of an infinite number of other reactions. The one thing we must never forget as we move through a divorce is this: no matter how you or I might feel to the contrary, we are not alone in this journey. Everyone in our immediate family is affected, to say nothing of grandparents, friends, and even shirt-tail cousins.

One evening in a men's divorce group, one of the men was commemorating the third year of his divorce. As he reflected on the most difficult parts and then reiterated how relieved he was to be out of the marriage, he ended with this comment: "In the beginning, there are those little moments of grace when you think how mellow it is to be out of this hassle. No more arguments. No more impossible standoffs; you know, the futility of it all. But then, maybe a couple months out of the house, you start to realize that as long as you live, you'll be a part of this family unit, by virtue of the fact of your children. For the first time in my life, I know what they mean by that saying, *blood is thicker than water*."

This man's clear perspective is a valuable insight for all of us—that *where there are children involved, there's a bond that we may hold forever.* Realizing that the children need their Dad, even though he might be living in another city, or even another country, is a sobering reality. And because they do need us, we may need to go through periods of negotiating visitation rights and working to create home environments of our own where our kids not only feel comfortable but also don't feel in conflict about the other parent.

In the idealized world, of course, there would be no domestic strife and no divorce. But that's not what this book is about. Living as we do in a world where divorce is all too prevalent, we would do well to look at the best ways through it—beginning with the re-alization that if there are children, we will share a bond for many, many years to come. We're still going to be raising the children together, and if we're determined to do that well, it will take a collaborative effort.

SUCCESSFUL COLLABORATIVE DIVORCE SPANS THE YEARS

A man attended his daughter's wedding twelve years after he di-vorced her mother. Prior to the wedding, he and his ex-wife had spoken on the phone, promising each other that while they were both attending the wedding there would be no *scenes* between them. This was a time of celebration, not a time for opening old wounds. What surprised him, though, was that when the band started playing at the reception, he had a profound yearning to dance with his ex. When he timidly walked up to her to ask, she smiled brightly and eagerly drew him out onto the dance floor. Later, she said, "I was so afraid you wouldn't ask me." It was not a reconciliation, he said, for they had both gone on with their lives, and both had remarried. But clearly, they felt the bond they shared through their daughter, and it felt good to acknowledge and celebrate it in this way. "I am so glad we were able to share this moment," he told his ex-wife.

This is the hope of collaborative divorce. To be able to support children in their important moments without excluding or alienating the other parent. To be friends. In so many ways, divorce—at least divorce involving children—is not ending a relationship but changing that relationship. Where children are concerned, Dad is still Dad and Mom is still Mom. Down the road, there may be stepparents who, at least partially, take on those roles, and may even be addressed by your children as Dad or Father. But the reality is that the genetic bonds you share with your children do not go away. Keeping that in mind, let this perspective guide you through the process of divorce, looking for ways to honor what will not go away and directing your efforts to protecting your children.

This book is here to help you understand how to move forward compassionately, composedly, and collaboratively. With a collection of stories taken from real experiences shared in men's groups and forums, combined with easy and logical advice and rules, you'll find your own way to being the World's Best Dad after divorce.

CHAPTER ONE:

THE BREAKING POINT

"Divorce is one of the loneliest of modern rituals."
—*Suzanne Gordon*

ONE LAST TRY

Maybe, just maybe, you're not quite ready to call it quits. You're both talking about breaking up, and you've gone through a few periods of reconciliation, but no papers have been signed and no property agreements have changed hands. Is it worth one last try? Statistically, once she or you have stepped over that particular threshold, there is little chance of getting back together. It's a big step, and not one that is easily reversed.

Let's say you're at least still sharing the same house, however-er tension-filled it might be. Is it worth it to try counseling? If you're not in counseling already and you are sincere about giving the marriage one last try, seriously consider it. Talk it over with your partner, letting her know that you would very much like to enter counseling, since you want to stay married to her. Bear in mind, however, that professional help can be a great asset only if both you and your spouse are equally committed to working it out, with the goal of staying married. You may have doubts and fears. That's only human. But you want to stay together in spite of how uncomfortable you both feel about the changes you are facing.

Will you be plagued with doubts along the way? Of course. In the haunting hours between midnight and 3 a.m., who does not fall prey to the ghosts of perplexity and skepticism? If you find your doubts and fears keeping you awake at night, or distract-ing you during the day, you might even want to consider private therapy, just for you, in addition to the work you might be doing together with a marriage counselor.

While people have shared many stories with me about how counseling brought their relationship back together, there are also stories of breakups that have been helped during divorce through counseling.

These, too, are success stories—though the successes were measured in a slightly different way. For example, in a men's group, formed to help recently divorced fathers, one man confessed, "My wife had to drag me into counseling kicking a screaming. I made some effort to participate, but I never was really into it. I knew it was over, and I wanted out more than I've ever wanted anything in my life. Looking back on it, though, I'm really glad I went. It helped both of us work through some of the fears we had about ending it, and we were able to actually help each other in the separation. Today, we're good friends. We've been able to cooperate really well where the kids are concerned, and that's something both of us consider valuable. I don't think we could have gotten to this place as fast as we did had it not been for those last sessions with the shrink."

Because separating can be so complicated, many couples go through a trial separation before making their final decision. Do trial separations really work? Usually, by the time a couple has gotten this far, it's pretty likely that they'll eventually go on to make the separation permanent. But the fact of the matter is that once in a great while, given some time apart, a couple will reassess their own complaints and shortcomings, have a better perspective on what it would really mean to be divorced, and so will be motivated by this time apart to work a little harder to get back together.

A trial separation can be difficult where the kids are concerned, however. What do you tell them? Since you can't actually promise your kids that you'll reconcile, better to give them something solid they can deal with. Just assure them that, "Even though Dad is going to have a place of his own now, he's still your dad, he'll always be your dad. You'll continue to see a lot of him, and you'll also have another home where you can go to be with him." Assuring the kids that while things are changing, you'll always be their dad helps them deal with their primary fear—that maybe you won't love them anymore.

Assuming that you are determined to do a trial separation, be sure that you jointly decide upon a time period. Between six and twelve months is reasonable. But be specific. Set a date, and make certain it's by mutual agreement. After that time, you can take a look at your situation, perhaps with the help of your marriage counselor or therapist, and then decide what your next move is going to be.

If this is to be a trial separation, be very clear that you both understand what this means. You are still married to each other. If you get emotionally and sexually involved with another person, it's no longer a trial separation. You've moved on to explore other relationships. Time does heal wounds caused by unfaithfulness, but if you're sincere about a trial separation, you'll realize early on that this is not a time to open up new wounds.

TELLING THE KIDS

Let's assume that either you decided not to have a trial separation or the separation did not serve to bring you back together. You've both made up your mind—or at least one of you is very adamant about ending the marriage—and it's time to press on. The first order of business is going to be telling the kids.

In an ideal world, Mom and Dad would sit down together with the kids and, in an orderly and compassionate way, tell them what was going on. However, at this point in your divorce, usually one or both parents are feeling anxious and confused. No matter how you feel, you're simply going to have to move forward, and to do that, you're going to need to pull yourself together. While each family situation is going to be somewhat different, here are some of the basic questions you'll need to address with your spouse, and all of them will directly or indirectly affect your kids.

• How do we go about calling a truce?

- Where do we go for the professional advice that will make this transition easier?

- What do we need to do to be able to sit down together and tell the kids about our divorce?

- Who will be moving out?

- Where will the kids live?

- How will money issues be resolved?

- What do the kids already know about the breakup?

- What do the kids still need to know about the breakup?

CALLING A TRUCE

This is a big one. You still have many unresolved differences between you. Maybe you're feeling raw and hurt, with wounds that require very little to reopen. Even so, once you've made the decision to divorce, there's business to attend to that is going to require strength that you may have never imagined that you possess. For your children, you've got to step back, survey what's got to be done, and then move on to creating a new path for your new family situation. This is where true collaboration begins, with both of you making an agreement with each other to call a truce, an end to active fighting.

Most people handle this part of the divorce best by seeking the help of their marriage counselor, if they have one. In this case, it's not marriage counseling you need, but collaborative divorce counseling. Your mission is to maintain the truce so that you can sit down with the kids and tell them what's going on. This is not about you or how you feel; it is about your kids. This moment will stay with them forever, so be prepared to put your hurt and anger aside and focus on what they need.

GETTING PROFESSIONAL ADVICE

Collaborative divorce depends on your recognizing when you can use experienced help and when it's okay to go it alone. Above all, don't be the victim of false pride—exercising the *I can do this myself* approach that's the target of so much male bashing. At this stage of the journey, you're best off looking for the shortest and easiest route through all of this, with minimal damage inflicted upon anyone and everyone who might be involved. The good news is that there are experienced professionals out there who can be tremendously helpful. Having an unbiased third party involved will make communication with your spouse much easier, increasing the ability to resolve issues. You've got to face the fact that if you were able to sort out your problems on your own, you would not now be divorcing. This is not a judgment of you or your spouse, by the way, since every one of us has individual differences, and when we put two or more people together, those differences can either complicate our communication or make it easier. In a divorce, the issue is nearly always the former.

A word of caution: your friends are not professional counselors, and you shouldn't treat them as such. Most of us in times of crisis—and divorce is almost always a crisis—seek out the comfort and solace of our friends. Be careful not to put your friends in a position of having to take sides, particularly if it's a mutual friend of yours and your spouse. You'll quickly burn them out if they feel in this conflicted position.

Stay focused. Keep in mind that you are not in therapy to get back together with your spouse. Yes, it does happen now and then as the partners start the divorce process, but nevertheless, don't confuse psychotherapy with divorce counseling. What you are doing here is resolving core issues that will have serious long-term effects on your children and their mother. Your goal is to create a way of being with your soon-to-be ex-spouse that will be healthy for your kids.

LEAVE THE LAWYER STUFF FOR LATER

In the midst of the initial breakup, most people have a tendency to believe they must immediately seek out an attorney and start filing for divorce. You might be feeling that this is the way to reduce the confusing feelings you are experiencing, that once you've filed, you'll feel much relieved. Trust me, it generally doesn't work that way. My advice is this: while you and your ex, or soon-to-be ex, are rather volatile emotionally—which is normal—you should not be trying to make any big decisions. Wait until you start to feel more solid. The only exception to this is that you might want to get an hour's consultation with an attorney to get any questions you might have answered. What are some of the questions you might wish to ask? Here's a good list for starters:

- Custody rights: what's customary? What is possible given any special circumstances you might have, such as your moving to another city or another state?

- How will community property be divided?

- What about support payments for your children?

- How will the divorce affect your taxes?

You may be able to calculate, on the basis of this meeting, how the divorce is going to impact your finances. In this way, you'll be able to gain a realistic idea of how your situation changes.

TELLING THE KIDS TOGETHER

There is no easy way to do this. Just do your best with it, and when in doubt, bet on the truth. It's best for the kids if you tell them together, at the same time, but make certain you and Mom agree to this ahead of time and even talk over how it's going to go.

If you're feeling very unsure, seek help from a marriage counselor. This can greatly reduce your own anxiety about telling the kids and will give you some guidelines to follow. You'll need to tell them in a way that is realistic in terms of their age. If your kids are of different ages, you'll need to speak to them in a way that is understandable for them all.

Whatever you do, after you explain to the kids about the changes that are about to happen, take each child aside separately and address their individual concerns and needs. Encourage them to ask questions and to express what they are feeling. Answer their questions in a way that will not put down their mother in any way. And take the time to acknowledge their feelings without dissecting them or trying to talk them out of it. For example, if your daughter tells you she is "sad and angry and scared all at the same time," let her know that you understand why she would feel that way, that she may feel that way for a while, but it will get better. If they're angry at you, answer, "I'm sure you are angry, sweetheart. I'm sorry that you feel this way, but I understand why you do right now. I still love you very much, and that will never change."

When my wife and I split up, each of our three kids was told at different times and places, and it did not take a lot of time for them to express their reaction or ask questions, which was a mistake. My eight-year-old son was confused by the way we told him. Both his mom and I held him in our laps in such a loving way that he thought something wonderful was about to happen. When we explained that his mom and I were getting a divorce, it didn't make sense to him. He couldn't put together the loving nurturing and the shocking news of the divorce. When we handled it that way, I now realize, we made it harder for the kids sort through their feelings.

It would have been better if I'd told my son that his mom and I needed to talk to him about some changes, and then took him with us to a quiet place. I could have told him that his mom and I realized that we were better at being friends than being married, but there is no greater joy for us than to be his parents. But to help him be happier, because we'd be happier, I would be getting a new house, and we'd have two homes for him and his brother and sister.

Regardless of how you choose to tell your kids, do so in a way that is sensitive to their individual needs, in an age-appropriate manner, with your actions and words expressing a coherent message.

Telling the kids won't be easy. There's no way to avoid some upset—yours and theirs. Keep the above in mind and be as aware as you possibly can of your children's reactions. The better you pay attention to their expressions and words, the better you'll be able to handle any difficulties they may be having with it, now and in the future.

WHO MOVES OUT OF THE HOME

In most cases, it's the father who moves out of the family home. The main reason for this is to minimize the changes in the children's lives, assuming that Mom was the primary caretaker and is granted full or shared custody. From the kids' point of view, it is difficult enough to have a parent move out. Make sure that whether it's Mom or Dad who becomes the primary caregiver, that you maintain the home base, which gives the kids a sense of familiarity and security. This is not always possible, of course, since families may have to downsize to a smaller home, move to another neighborhood or city, or otherwise change residence as a result of the divorce. But whatever life necessitates, don't ever lose sight of how important it is for children to have the security of a place that feels like home.

Whoever leaves the home will have to deal with the kids' perception that you are the one ending the marriage. Telling the truth is important to your relationship with your kids. If you are the one moving out, be up front about your feelings in a loving way. Their mom is not the "bad guy" or kicking you out, but still express that you hate to leave them.

MONEY, MONEY, MONEY, MONEY

Money will be a major issue in most cases, especially for single-income families. If you are the main breadwinner in the family, you'll have to support two households—yours and hers. Clearly, this can be a major financial burden for most people and may necessitate some big changes in your lifestyle. This alone may stir up feelings of frustration, anxiety, and anger.

This is the point at which many men withdraw and even abandon their fathering responsibilities. As much as this might be a temptation—"to just cut and run," as one man put it—hang on. Don't bail out on your responsibilities. Sure, you're going to have to do some belt-tightening. And, yes, it's going to get to you that your ex has a more comfortable place to live than you do *and* she's got the kids. But the kids are the ones to focus on, not her. The sacrifices you make are for their comfort.

I'm not going to try to paint a pretty picture here. You know the truth of your situation only too well, and nothing I can tell you at this point is going to make money matters much easier. But once again, you'll need to remind yourself to keep your kids on the top of your priority list. Be available to them emotionally. Show up for them 100 percent.

One of the biggest shocks men face in the first months of their divorce is how radically their relationship changes with their ex. Suddenly, money becomes the main focus of virtually every interaction between you. You'll wonder what happened to the person you once loved and who loved you. Why is it now only about the bucks?

And what about her? She'll be amazed at your seeming indifference to her needs. There's a great distance between you now; maybe even a wall that neither of you can scale.

Does it get any better? Sure. It does, but only if you work at it rather than sinking into self-pity, chaos, revenge, and victimization. What I and others have found is that divorcing and living apart imposes perhaps as many demands as being together; though the issues are different and maybe less embroiled. But clearly, making a divorce work is rivaled only by making a marriage work, a challenge that's compounded when there are kids involved.

WHAT THE KIDS KNOW
ABOUT THE BREAKUP

Our first reflex is to spare the kids the details of the divorce. However, this is not always wise. If there has been a lot of tension between the parents, the kids will have experienced it. You're hiding nothing from them. And, obviously, if there have been other overt problems, such as emotional and physical violence, mental illness, or drug or alcohol abuse, the kids will already be aware of this, no matter what their ages. They will often feel great relief when the conflict stops. If those kinds of problems have been going on, let your children know that, with the divorce, this behavior will stop and that they need not feel tense and anxious thereafter.

Always tell your kids any news about the divorce in an age-appropriate manner. Young children won't understand the same issues as the older kids, of course, so you need to frame your conversations with them so that they can grasp what's happening.

Don't lie to your kids in an effort to protect them or yourself. Even children who appear to only have the most modest grasp of language often can determine what's truth and what's not. Remember, when in doubt, place your bets on the truth.

KIDS' IMMEDIATE REACTION

You can count on the kids reacting in a variety of different ways depending on their age and level of maturity—sometimes all within a matter of minutes. Be prepared for this and know that the best medicine for it at this time is to allow them to have their feelings, regardless of what they might be. They are providing you with the information you'll need over the next few months to give them the support they'll be needing. Here is a list of what you might expect:

- Relief from the fighting and arguments between their parents.

- Withdrawal and disbelief.

- Shock, anger, and crying.

- Worry about how their lives will change.

- Anger at one or both parents.

- Anger at you because you are leaving—they may even blame you.

- Shame and embarrassment.

- Confusion about loyalty to one or the other parent.

- Bewilderment about who to believe when the parents disagree.

- Guilt—believing they may be to blame for the breakup.

Even when children seem to accept the news and changes fairly well, be alert to changes in their emotions as the new reality continues to sink in.

As much as you may want to ease your kids' and your own pain at this point, there really is nothing you can do to rush the healing that must take place. It's here that the old Taoist saying, "Don't push the river, it flows by itself" becomes the rule of the day. But while healing takes time, there are things you can say that will help your kids through the transition, keeping them in a place of relative safety as they negotiate this new territory. Here are six key concepts that you'll want to convey to your kids. Don't drag out your discussion of these points, but make certain you keep it clear, simple, and age-appropriate.

1. Assure them the divorce is not their fault and that they are not in any way responsible for Mom and Dad wanting to live in different houses.

2. Tell them often that you love them.

3. Assure them that even though you are not living in the same house with them, you will not ever abandon them.

4. Tell them you're sorry to have caused this mess.

5. Instruct them to be patient, that many other kids have gone through this, just as they are doing now, and eventually it will get easier and they will feel "normal" again.

6. Tell them that even though Mom and Dad are no longer living together that you are all still *family* and that will never change.

This final point is perhaps the greatest concern of many children; they no longer feel like they have a family. This feeling of divorce for the whole family can cause kids to act out or seek belonging in peer groups outside the home, which can bring its own problems.

THE BREAKING POINT   21

DECIDE TO BE THE
BEST DAD YOU CAN BE

In the months that you'll be making these changes in your life, you'll no doubt be encountering a great deal of confusion and emotional upheaval. You'll probably be feeling every emotion imaginable, running the spectrum from anger to fear, relief, and deep sadness. All that being so, hold the intention uppermost in your mind that regardless of whatever else is going on, you'll be the best father that you can possibly be. No matter what you are dealing with, you will keep your kids' mental, emotional, spiritual, and physical health at the top of your priority list.

As you try to adjust to your new normal, your direct involvement may not always be in your children's best interest. Brent, whose daughter was five years old when he divorced her mother, told the story of how, soon after leaving the family home and finding an apartment for himself, he felt literally overcome by anxiety and depression. The first time he was supposed to have little Shelly for the weekend, he called up and canceled.

"I just couldn't do it," he said. "I was a total basket case." Taking Shelly in that state wouldn't have been good for her. However, in his own mind, this was a big failure as a dad, and his first reaction was to just withdraw entirely from his daughter's life.

"Fortunately," he said. "I had a friend who'd been through a similar thing. She told me not to beat myself up for not seeing Shelly that weekend. I should still hold my intention and do my level best to get myself together."

Brent did exactly that, and except for times when he was out of town on business, he kept his weekend visits with his daughter. Ultimately, he did become the kind of father he wanted to be, and while there were difficulties over the years, he was able to keep a loving and caring focus on her.

Recognize that you will fail now and then to live up to the ideals you've committed to in being a father, but don't judge yourself on the basis of an occasional miss. Just pick yourself up again, restate your intention, and go on.

CHAPTER TWO:

THE GROUND RULES FOR COLLABORATIVE DIVORCE

"Start by doing what's necessary; then do what's possible,
and suddenly, you are doing the impossible."
—*St. Francis of Assisi*

When I got to this chapter in the book, I made a conscious decision to write a short, easy-to-follow chapter, with no frills, that would lay out the ground rules for collaborative divorce. So that's what you'll find here. However, it is intended that you read these pages from the viewpoint that is the rules are intended only as a way of articulating core issues you might encounter. There are no hard-and-fast rules; but there is a boundary that we should all respect—that each of us is a human being with our own unique set of strengths and weaknesses. As such, we deserve each other's mutual respect, regardless of what battles we might face.

Yes, mutual respect is necessary, for no better reason than to make things easier on your children. So long as they are in the picture, you and your ex will have a relationship, even though it is now different. And some of the same issues you had when you were together are going to carry over. Here, you are faced with having to coordinate responsibilities involving the kids—everything from signing them up for out-of-school activities to saving for a college education or for other training that interests them. Some of these issues can be pretty highly charged, too, and the best way through them is to establish some ground rules ahead of time. That's what collaborative divorce is all about.

As you read this book, bear in mind that following these guidelines, alone or along with your ex-spouse, will make life easier for everyone involved. If you are the only one implementing them, have patience. In time, these practices will rub off on your ex—as well as your kids, by the way—as they all begin to reap the benefits.

I'm not promising that any of this will be easy. It might, in fact, be quite hard in the beginning. Have patience, give it time, and things will improve.

THREE COMMUNICATIONS SCENARIOS

In the heat of addressing emotional issues, logic and reason often take a back seat—or never even get on board. It's easy to recognize when another person's emotions are overriding good sense, less easy to recognize when it's happening to us. When you're facing a stressful situation with your ex, remind yourself to let go of any illusions you might have of managing others' emotions and put your efforts into managing your own. Your ability to manage your emotions will determine which of the following three communication styles you will exhibit with your ex.

- You regularly have civil discussions with your ex.

- You and your ex can have limited civil discussions but it doesn't take much to go into a major meltdown

- You can't talk at all without really losing it.

At any given time, we all fit into one of the above categories. While we would like to have a civil discussion, in most cases we are not able to. That's where the guidelines become most helpful. Take the time to look over the above three styles and be honest with yourself about determining which category you fit into at the moment. Then, build skills, using this book, to help you move from wherever you are now to a point where you and your ex can work more collaboratively.

TEN BASIC RULES FOR COMMUNICATIONS TOOLS

- Remember to Be Nice

- The 24-Hour Rule

- Spare the Kids

- Don't Burden the Kids with Your Pain

- Third-Party Help

- Create Clear Boundaries

- Asking for What You Want

- Let Her Have Her Way While Not Giving Up Yours

- Listen to Her Complaints without Defending Yourself

- Finding Ways to Agree

Remember to Be Nice: This is the time to try hard to be nice and polite. Often, a look, an off-hand remark, or a gesture will send you or your ex into an attack or defensive mode. Resist this reaction. Sometimes, something as simple as putting your hand on your stomach will ground you and calm you down enough so you can just relax a bit and concentrate on having a civil conversation.

Establish the 24-Hour Rule: There is usually a period of negotiation in any divorce, when both parties are working out what they need and what they can live with. The 24-Hour Rule is an easy way to avoid making impulsive mistakes.

It's simple: Any time you are faced with a decision, insist on taking twenty-four hours to think about it. When you know you have this cushion, it's much easier to handle any emotions triggered by that proposition. Most issues around divorce are hot in the beginning, so having this cushion gives you assurance that you'll have time to think things out and even do a little research. It'll minimize the error of making agreements just to end the hassle, and then regretting what you did later on. The 24-Hour Rule gives everyone an elegant and easy way out.

I know when I was pressed to made important on the spot decisions while feeling angry, hurt, or vulnerable, I'd agree to things just to end the hassle and wound up becoming resentful about the decision. In the early stages of my divorce, I had real trouble dealing with immediate challenges.

Spare the Kids: You don't want the kids to take sides and/or be in the middle of the hassles. It's best that while you are rebuilding your relationship, you are at least civil to each other, and that you do this even when the children are not present. While this might take some effort, your peace of mind will increase knowing you are sparing the kids from this stressful re-connecting.

Don't Burden the Kids with Your Pain: While this may seem like a repetition of the last rule, it is important to emphasize this point. When communicating with your ex, if you are angry and hurt, don't release your frustration on the kids. Don't tell them how much your ex is making you crazy or hurt. They don't need to know the specifics of infidelity, of abuse, or any of the other things that would wound the children to hear. This is hard to avoid, but, take it from me, it will only come back and cause everyone pain, especially the kids. You do not want your children to be held hostage and injured in an uncivil war.

Third-Party Help: If all you can manifest is shouting, slamming of doors, and hanging up of phones, it might be time for some third-party help. A third party can help you get past the emotions and establish the new ground rules for collaborating. One suggestion would be to hire a family therapist to help. This is often called post-divorce advice. It is cheaper than a lawyer, and it will, in most cases, reduce the time spend having the lawyers haggling details out.

Create Clear Boundaries: This is very important. If you don't draw a line in the sand regarding what type of treatment you will accept now, how will she ever know how you feel and think about issues? The fact that you are divorcing concludes that neither one of you have a good understanding of what makes each other tick, or what ticks each other off. It is now time for you to express how you want to be treated and accept nothing less than that. What do you have to lose? After all, you are divorcing.

Ask for What You Want: Dovetailing with the previous rule, be clear about what you want! Rather than being defensive, holding out, or having her have to guess what you really want, practice saying and asking for what you want. If you want the kids more often, want to take your favorite easy chair from the house, need her to be more patient when you are trying to formulate your thoughts, or whatever, be calm and just say what you want and need. You might not get it, but you can ask. This is another good place to bring in the 24-Hour Rule. Ask her to think about it for twenty-four hours before deciding against your wishes, and gently point out the times when you have given into her wishes. This is what collaboration is all about.

Let Her Have Her Way While Not Giving Up Yours: This can be difficult, but life is full of trade-offs and compromises. But if you act graciously with the small problems, in most cases, you will have some bargaining power when it comes to issues that really mean something to you. I am not recommending that you simply give up things that you want and are important to you, because that will only make you resentful and angry. However, I am suggesting that you don't sweat the small stuff. Listen to what is important to her, and acknowledge that you may have conflicting interests, but working together to find common ground will make every other interaction easier.

Listen to Her Complaints without Defending Yourself:
This is a constant and reoccurring theme. Often, we cannot bring ourselves to actually listen to what our ex is saying because we are angry and self-absorbed in our own wants, defenses, and desires. Whether or not we are justified in our position is not the issue. The issue now is to create clear and easy communications that gets the job done. The best way to be proactive in this regard is to be a good listener. The only way to really listen is to not be defending your position while she is complaining about you or your actions.

Not defending yourself does not mean giving into something that you don't agree with. It does mean not reacting to the hot buttons that will naturally be pushed when she is complaining about you. At this point, it is best to evoke the 24-Hour Rule. Just say that you need twenty-four hours to consider anything and you don't want to react out of emotion before you answer. This will give both you and her a cooling off period.

And there is another side of the same coin, something just as important. Throughout the marriage, no doubt there have been things you have wanted to change about your wife. Now that the marriage is over, those same things are probably still bugging you as you try to work out the details of post-divorce life. You could not change her then. Do not make plans or try to change her now. Accept, and even honor, her right to be who she is. You can't control her behavior, but you can always control yours. Remember to be polite while establishing these boundaries.

Find Ways to Agree: If you can quickly agree on minor hassles, then, when major hassles come up that are really stressful to manage, you both have built a pattern of cooperating and can fall back and make an agreement that works toward a more permanent foundation for communication. So, try to find things to agree on and remind each other about those, rather than focusing on the things that don't work. For example, agree you both love the kids and want the best for them.

SWITCHOVER DAY STRESS

During the early years, switchover day is the worst day of the week, especially for the younger kids. I remember my young son often calling me Mom several times after I picked him up from his mother's house, causing him embarrassment. It's difficult as they go from one house to another house where the rules are somewhat different, and so is the food. There is also the potential for sadness and anger for the kids, and for you.

Consider these things to help simplify what is confusing or exacerbating.

Dropping Off and Picking Up the Kids: It's best to hand off the younger kids directly to the other parent. If age-appropriate and you're not getting along civilly with your former wife, it is best to drop the kids outside her house or arrange to drop them at school and have the other parent pick them up at the end of the school day. Be clear with both your ex and the kids about the plan, and remind them the day of to clear up confusion.

Seeing Her, or Not Seeing Her: You must decide if you want to see your ex when you drop off the kids. There are a few reasons to not see her at switchover time:

- You're not getting along too well

- You can't stand her

- You long for her

- She longs for you

- Her boyfriend will answer her door

If you have an important message about the kids to deliver, you must do it. But if you're stressed about seeing her, perhaps you can phone or email the message before or after the switchover. The most important aspect is to not use this time to attack your ex or seek revenge or approval. Got it?

ESTABLISH GROUND RULES
FOR MEETINGS

Meetings can be explosive, especially in the early days or when you're not getting along very well with each other. Open-hearted listening is what's called for here. You take the hero's journey now, even though you have hurt each other before, believe you hate each other, don't trust each other, and/or have never attempted unprejudiced or non-defensive listening. Using the following list to create ground rules will help to ease the process:

- Have a list or agenda to discuss and stick to it

- Start all discussions with appreciation

- Learn to repeat back what you have heard without editing it

- Put yourself in her shoes for a few minutes

- Find out what the other person wants

- Be clear about what you want

- Negotiate and compromise

- Don't divert by getting angry

- Don't throw in other issues or change the subject

- Have good manners

- Stay logical even if she points out the subject is getting off track

- Own your own faults and limitations as well pointing out hers

- Honor her strengths even if you see her faults

Making the Decisions: Yes, it's good to have ground rules for this, too.

- Arrive at one decision at a time

- Confirm the agreement

- Discuss how you will review the decision

- Allow time to review and change it

- Record your agreement, possibly through an email exchange

- Discuss how each of you might fall short, despite agreeing to the decision

- And how to catch yourselves from doing falling short

There are plenty of issues to decide and you're not going to handle everything in one sitting. It will likely be an ongoing process, so become accustomed to working together for the sake of the kids. Your relationship now will set the stage for your new family culture.

MAKE PEACE, NOT WAR

Recognize that the war is over and it's time to build the peace. Forget who's right, who's wrong, and who betrayed whom. Put your kids first. You can't fix the past at this point, but you can make the present and the future better or worse depending on your present actions. So, call a truce. Put your energy into the collaborative skills described in this book. Avoid rehashing what can only cause pain and anger. Put your own issues aside when communicating with your ex about the kids.

CHAPTER THREE:

CREATING YOUR NEW HOME

"A man travels the world over in search of what he needs,
and returns home to find it."
—George A. Moore

The decision has been made. You and your wife are going to separate. You may not be the one who initiated this parting of the ways, but you are very likely to be the person who leaves the family home. You might be looking forward to finally having some relief from the constant tension you've been experiencing for so long. But there are some tough realities to face as well. At the top of the list is the fact that, along with being separated from your wife, you're also going to be separated from your children.

You'll be seeing them, of course, but from now on, it will be mostly short visits—weekends, holidays, special occasions, and perhaps some school days. And while you will be encouraged to stay in touch, visit often, and have them stay with you in your home, the chances are that even telephone calls back and forth will have to be arranged ahead of time.

Most men who've been close to their kids find the first several months away from the family home filled with heartache and a sense of loss. You may find yourself in a constant debate with yourself: *Have I done the right thing? Have I missed something important here, something I might still be able to address with my ex? Will I lose the kids' love? What if my ex remarries, the kids get along really well with their stepdad, and they all ditch me? What are the kids thinking and feeling about me these days?*

Whatever else might be going through your mind at this time, keep reminding yourself that your main concern right now needs to be your kids. The more you are able to focus on them, the more you'll come into alignment with what's important and necessary. At the same time, remind yourself that this is a highly emotional time for all of you. There will be times when you scream at your ex, slam down the phone when she calls, storm around the house super pissed off and totally losing sight of the kids' needs. It's inevitably going to happen from time to time. Don't give yourself a bad time about it. You're only human. Just keep coming back to center, turning your healthy focus back to the kids' needs—and setting your sights on the ultimate goal of establishing a collaborative relationship with your ex.

First things first. You've got to have a place where your kids can feel at home, and that means making your new place feel like home to you. This may very well be a challenge since you're probably downsizing, living in a more modest place than your ex and the kids. If you're living in an apartment while your ex and your kids are in a home that is larger, and in a better neighborhood, it may take a while for both you and your kids to adjust. Older children, too, can become hyper-aware of these differences. If they have some anger and anxiety about your breakup—and it would be unusual for them not to—it may come out with their letting you know that you are not, at least in their eyes, *living up to their expectations.*

When Daniel divorced, he purchased a large, three-bedroom mobile home in a decent community at the edge of town. He had chosen this place not only because he could afford it, but also because it offered amenities he thought his daughter might enjoy. There was a swimming pool, a gym, a tennis court, and a nearby lake with sailboats and canoes. It was a tidy, well-kept community, with stunning flower gardens, thanks to a number of retirees living there. In spite of it all, Ibis, his fourteen-year-old daughter, was anything but impressed. She refused to stay overnight on her first visit. When Daniel dropped her off at her mother's, she turned to him and said, "I never dreamed my own father would become trailer trash." Daniel was stunned. He drove away feeling shamed and hurt.

By the end of the first summer, however, Ibis had discovered the swimming pool and tennis courts at the mobile home complex and had enrolled in a sailing class on the small lake less than a half-mile away. It had taken her a while to adjust, but soon she eagerly looked forward to visits with Dad, where there were more things to do than at her mom's.

I offer Daniel and Ibis' story to illustrate how kids can change and adjust. But there's a subtext in their story that shouldn't be passed over without comment since it reveals the hidden struggles kids often have in a divorce. Ibis was angry with her father for leaving her mother. In her mind, because he was the one who left the family home, he was to blame for the breakup. Years later, she'd express these feelings more openly, admitting that she had seen him as the culprit and, by her own admittance, had looked for ways to put him down. The "trailer trash" comment had been one of the ways she'd found to express her anger.

But Daniel's story also proves that it is possible to create comfort and even a touch of luxury on the kinds of budget constraints divorced parents sometimes face.

Children's emotions can be turbulent, particularly in the teens, and it may take some time for their perceptions to change about you and what you have to offer them. It's the patient dad, the dad who hangs in there, expressing his love, continuing to give his kids the best life he can provide, even when they seem totally unappreciative, who finally comes out on top, loved, and admired by his kids. It may take more time than you'd like, and you'll have to be careful about setting reasonable limits on their behavior as you guide them through the difficult first months of your divorce, but without this kind of love and caring, the kids can end up in tough shape indeed.

LOCATION, LOCATION, LOCATION

As I've said, the first months of a divorce are usually uncomfortable for all concerned, and it's natural to have moments when you want to run far, far away. But as millions of men have discovered, there is no quick escape from the feelings tumbling around in your mind at this time—and you know at the bottom of your heart that you just can't abandon your kids without consequences that will one day come back to bite you.

As you consider where to move, you'll have to consider your kids' access to school, activities, and friends. Kids *need* the stability of their usual routines and their friends during this time of transition. And make no mistake; they also need their mom to be easily accessible when they're with you.

Whenever possible, kids should have free and open access to both parents and to all other friends and relatives who have played an important part in their lives. Being within walking or biking distance of Mom's house is ideal for the kids. That close proximity is certainly going to minimize your need to taxi your kids back and forth. In addition, if you work full time, as most of us do, having your ex as backup can make your life much easier for you, though, obviously, this depends on your and her ability to collaborate.

For various reasons, however, this close proximity is not always possible. Joseph recalls the first months of his divorce, when he got an apartment just two blocks from his ex's home. Every time his ex needed a babysitter to go out on a date, or simply to go shopping, he was called to help.

"At first," he said, "I thought it would be good if I went over to the house and sat with my kids over there. But it was painful. Every time I walked in the front door, I was confronted with my memories of the hard times I'd spent there. Then, about three months after we filed for divorce, my ex brought in her 'new friend' to introduce him to me. I wasn't ready for that! I just had to stop going over there. Then the kids came to my place, which was just a tiny studio apartment, and it was just too cramped for all of us. Besides, frankly, I didn't want to be that close and see her comings and goings. And until I was ready to be meeting her new friends, I had to protect myself. Finally, I moved across town to a new place in a great neighborhood with much more space and a yard where the kids are welcome to play. It's not ideal, I suppose, but I'm more comfortable and the kids have their own rooms. They actually seem to like it better than our previous arrangement, but I think that's because it's more like a home for me, too."

Of course, life doesn't always cooperate in the ways you'd wish. Your job or your ex's job may require you to move away from your kids. Maybe your ex needs more support with caregiving from family. This could mean that you (or they) will move a few miles away or across the country, which will complicate spending time with your kids. You'll have to make arrangements for them to visit you or for you to visit them. There's always the phone, and if you can't get together with them for weekends, make sure you contact them regularly—at least once or twice a week. If you can afford it, and your kids can be trusted to use it responsibly, consider paying for their own phone.

While regular contact by phone is certainly helpful, don't think it's a substitute for actual contact with you. Budget your time and your money so that you can visit them, or have them visit you as often as humanly possible. Proving with your actions that no distance can keep you from your children will help you strengthen your relationship with your children.

Location can prove tricky, no matter the actual distance. But when you prioritize your children's needs, find a way to make your new house a home, and are determined to maintain quality contact in person or over the phone, you can overcome the separation, no matter the miles. Work with your ex to establish a schedule and an easy access for the kids to reach out to both Mom and Dad.

Mom and Dad both reap the benefits of a good collaboration since the kids come out happy and well-adjusted, certain in their own minds that they are still loved, in spite of the fact that their parents no longer live together. They still have a family where they feel loved and supported. The family was not broken; it was extended.

MAKE ROOM FOR THE KIDS

I have known several men who, faced with the realities of being single again, have rented small studios or one-bedroom apartments with great views or particularly desirable locations. It's certainly human enough, wanting a place with ambience. But where are the kids going to fit in? Sure, they can camp out on your living room floor in their sleeping bags. That can even be fun for them . . . for a while. Then, they'll start getting the message that you really aren't making room for them in your new life.

If you can possibly afford it, your kids should have a room in your home. If they are teenagers of different genders, each should have a room of their own. Can't afford that kind of rent, plus your child support? There are usually ways of working it out, even with limited space. Use your ingenuity with the goal in mind that you want your children to feel that you are doing your very best to make a comfortable place for them in your life. Above all, you want to send them the message, through your actions, words, and deeds, that you treasure them and that you put time and energy and thought into their well-being wherever you are living.

Physical space can be as important as psychological space at this time. Most kids need a certain amount of privacy where their possessions are safe. If all you can manage is a single closet or a footlocker for your child's belongings, do that. In a small living space, a throw rug and a cabinet or dresser for your child's clothes and toys can give them the sense of privacy and ownership that says, "This is my space. I have a place here, and I want you to respect it." Do, in fact, respect that space as your child's. Make it very clear to your child that this is their space, and have them fully participate in creating it by choosing what they're going to put there. Never make the mistake of absently sticking something of your own there without asking. It may be convenient to use the top drawers of your child's dresser for bills and your checkbook material, but if that's truly the only place you can find for them, be sure you get permission first.

Well, that's all great, but what about me? you may be asking at this point. Your creature comforts are important. If this place doesn't feel like your home, your children are going to pick that up almost immediately. Whatever house or apartment you choose should be a pleasant place for you, somewhere you'll feel good coming back to every night. The fact is, you'll be spending more time there than you might expect. Fix it up so that it pleases you and the kids. Bring in your favorite chair from your previous home, pictures on the walls that you enjoy, records, family photos, books, an entertainment center. Being surrounded by familiar objects helps to make a strange apartment or house a home. You will find comfort in this way, and your kids will, too.

Comforting yourself is important. Make certain that you have around you the things that allow you to feel connected, creative, and up. This is an excellent time to take stock of who you are and what you want from life. Where do you want to be five years from now? Ten years? Think about what's ahead of you and make plans about what you'll do to get there.

WHAT'S COOKIN'?

At this point in human evolution, gender roles have broken down for most of us. More men than ever are cooking, for example, and in a great many families, they cook most of the family meals. At the same time, we're a society of fast foods and convenience foods. Our kids are growing fat on hamburgers and French fries. In the beginning, you may find yourself taking your kids out for a special *treat* at the closest fast-food joint, partly to get through meals as quickly and easily as possible, but also as a way of saying, "this is our special time together." This is okay for a while, but don't make it a way of life with your kids. Mealtime is an especially important time. When your kids see you cooking for them, or you invite them to help you prepare a meal, you are sending them a solid message that you care about them in this special way. When you sit down to eat with your kids, it's a time to talk and exchange information about your day. It's an excellent way to find out what's happing with each other.

If you don't know how to cook anything more than soup, beans, and hamburgers, start there. Do whatever you know how to do and then, expand your repertoire.

If you don't already know what your kids like to eat, find out. Ask your ex, if she is the one who did most of the shopping and meal preparation. Involve your children in the shopping as well as the cooking, remembering that children of today are prime targets for advertising, and the food that gets the biggest ad budgets is often loaded with sugar. So, yeah, whether you like it or not, you're going to need to look at issues like what's good and what's not so good for your children to be eating. All of this means that you'll need to start paying attention to nutrition and expanding your skills in the kitchen.

EXCUSE ME! DO I LOOK
LIKE A TAXI CAB?

Well, the answer to that question, from the vantage point of a nine-year-old who needs to get to soccer at 9 a.m. every Saturday morning, across town to his friend James' house for a birthday party at 1, and then back to Mom's by 7 p.m. because Grandma is coming to visit, yes, you do look like a taxi. And except for the hour and a half that you'll be watching soccer practice, most of the time you're going to have with your kid that day is in the car as you ferry him or her from place to place. It's not exactly what comes to mind when you hear the phrase "spending quality time with your children," but it'll have to do for this day.

Whether you have primary custody of your kids or they're with you only on weekends, transportation may well become a big part of your parental duties. The worst of it is that you'll need to juggle your own schedule around theirs. Are you all alone in this venture? Not necessarily. You and your kids may already be part of a carpool, with parents cooperatively joining together to share these responsibilities. You'll probably already know if your kids are already enrolled in a carpool, and if you weren't the parent who did the driving, you'll have to find out the details from your ex.

If public transportation is available and your child is old enough to handle it alone, this can be a godsend. But before you encourage this, check out the route yourself. Go on an outing with your child, taking exactly the same route that he or she might later be taking alone, making sure that it is safe and is a trip your child can manage. If dependable taxi service is available in the area where you live, consider setting up an account with them to pick up and deliver your kids at certain times and on certain days. Over time, one particular taxi driver is usually assigned to your kids. This service can be expensive, but if your work schedule conflicts with pickup times, it can be well worth it.

Another alternative, if you have scheduling conflicts with your kids, is to hire a college student or retired person to do some of the driving. You might find a retired person who can pick up your kids, babysit them for an hour or more while you're still at work, and maybe even do a little grocery shopping for you from time to time.

Finally, most schools these days have after-school programs available. Look into what your child's school offers, for it can give you an extra hour or more to get from your work to school. These programs can be excellent or poor depending on the people who are supervising. The best of them try to balance playtime, help with homework, and socializing. Get permission from the principal to observe the program in action before you enroll your kids.

The after-school programs through public schools are not free, however, though many offer sliding fee schedules that can help out if you're in need. But don't be late in picking up your children in the evening. There's usually a significant extra charge for doing so—like $25 for the first late charge (more than ten minutes late), $50 for the next, and after that you're outta there for good.

Even with the best babysitter or after-school care, you'll have to schedule extra time for picking your kids up, maybe chatting with the teacher or other parents, or stopping at the convenience store on the way home and incidental little time-consuming extras you didn't anticipate.

STAYING THE COURSE

Nobody who's ever been through what we're exploring in this book ever claimed it is easy. It's not. The situation stinks; there's no doubt about it. And the most challenging part of it is trying to meet your kids' needs at a time when you are feeling anything but strong and sure. It's vital that you hold steady, nevertheless, to do your level best to manage each situation with patience and with your focus on your kids' well-being.

Put yourself in your kids' shoes. Think about how difficult it is for them as innocent victims of a situation they had no part in creating. Let them know that you know how hard it is on them. Assure them, however, that you're going to work it out and, in just a little while, things will start feeling a whole lot better for everyone—for them (the kids), for Mom, and for yourself. Tell the kids that even though you and their Mom no longer live under the same roof, you both still love them and will always be there for them. Your love for them won't stop just because you are building a new home. Reassure them that there is always room for them and that their needs are your highest priority.

It is during this time that other parents can become powerful allies. You may find a helpful cohort in your carpool or at the playground where your kids are practicing soccer on Saturday mornings. If you don't know it already, you'll soon discover that parents are great networkers, sharing resources such as rides to the park or to school. But it doesn't stop there. If your kid is having trouble at school, ask for advice from other parents on how to handle it. You won't always get easy fixes, but you'll get answers and support. Take care to cultivate easy-going and reciprocal friendships. Be diligent about paying back any favors extended to you, even if all you can offer at the time is a sincere thank-you, with the invitation to call on you if the person who helped you needs a hand.

As soon as you feel able, reach out to your former wife and let her know that you will do everything in your power to establish a positive collaboration with her, particularly where the kids are involved. When you have the kids for an extended stay, be sure to report back to her how they did, how they ate, whether or not they had any difficulties that you think she should know about. Be sure to report the good things that happened, not just the problems. And never, ever imply that somehow her parenting was to blame. Create and build, always with the faith that your positive and supportive efforts will strengthen your kids and allow them to feel good about themselves.

If you have difficult moments with your kids as they adjust to their new home life, and they share their discomfort about what they are feeling, give them something to build on, to have faith in. Explain to them that just like a bruise or other hurt, the discomfort or pain they are now feeling will, in time, go away. Let them know that if they want to tell you how they are feeling, you will do your best to listen *carefully* and try to make things better. Let them know that they are not alone in having divorced parents. Nobody finds it easy, but everyone makes it through.

CHAPTER FOUR:

NEW EXPECTATIONS FOR THE DAILY ROUTINE

"A schedule defends from chaos and whim."
—*Annie Dillard*

At this point, the die is cast. You have launched your new life and are facing the everyday realities of organizing your time as a single dad. At its simplest, the day should go something like this:

- 6:15: Alarm goes off, giving you time to shower, shave, and get yourself ready for the day before waking up the kids. Somewhere in there you start the coffee, put breakfast stuff on the table, and toss some dirty laundry in the washer.

- 6:45: Wake up the kids and get them ready for school. If the kids are younger, it will probably require some cajoling on your part and occasionally, stepping in to matching the right color socks, helping them with a pullover, and finding the sneaker which the dog decided to hide in the cat's litter box the night before.

- 7:15: Supervise breakfast while getting lunches packed and make sure books and other school materials are in their backpacks. While you're doing this, you are eating your own breakfast, drinking your coffee, etc.

- 7:40: Off to school. You're either driving them yourself or taking them down to the curb to be picked up by the bus or driving group you belong to.

- 8:00: If the kids were picked up at home, you might take this opportunity to take a deep breath. And while you are doing that, you might be quickly cleaning up the kitchen. You then gather your stuff together, and you're off to work. No matter your commute, it'll probably be in a mad rush.

- 9:00 to 5:00: You're at work. During the day, your ex calls you because she just received the medical insurance bill for the kids, and it's overdue. You handle it between work responsibilities. At 5:00, you make a mad dash for the parking lot. You've got a thirty-minute commute, on a good day, and the babysitter who picked the kids up from school at 3:30 needs your kids out of her house by 5:40 at the latest, so that she can start dinner for her husband and two teenaged daughters.

- 5:40: You've picked up the kids and are on your way home, but your son reminds you that you are out of milk and bread, so you stop at the convenience store, which means that you arrive home at just a bit past 6:00.

- 6:15: You cook some hamburgers and make a quick salad.

- With dinner over at 6:45, the kids get to watch a half-hour of TV while you clear away the dinner rubble and stick some dishes in the washer. It's then you remember you put some things in the washer before you left home that morning. You toss those things in the dryer and make a quick cruise through the kids' room, straightening up the worst of the mess before returning to the living room, shutting off the TV, and getting the kids to break out their homework.

- 8:45: The children are all snug in their beds. Ahhh,, a bit of time to yourself. It's delicious, but you're exhausted. By 9:40, you're sound asleep on the couch.

Those are how things work on the good days. Then, there are the not-so-good days, the days when everything that possibly could go wrong, does.

ON LESS THAN IDEAL DAYS

One winter morning, you and the kids leave your cozy apartment to go out to the freezing cold car and you discover your battery is dead. Road service is backed up for two hours. You frantically call people on your networking list. Turns out the only person who can help is your ex. She gives you a lecture about keeping your car in better shape but, on the plus side, she's willing to get the kids to school.

You have two children, but their after-school activities are on opposite sides of town today. The hired driver broke his leg and can't transport one of the kids. You decide to let the older child, newly licensed to drive, to use your car while you take the city bus, but your car gets a flat tire and your oldest is stranded halfway to their practice.

Work requires you to meet with a client in the early afternoon. But the client is late. And has a hundred questions. The meeting goes late, and you get involved in saving the account, not realizing that you're late to pick up your daughter, take her to her dentist appointment, or meet the babysitter who has your youngest.

Ideal days are in short supply in the early days, but how could they not be? Everyone is adjusting. You're soon hit with the reality that organizing the daily routine involves much more than keeping a calendar. In fact, the happiest solution you can imagine right now is that the gods will look down upon you and magically provide you with a social-director-psychotherapist-driver-babysitter-teacher all rolled into one. As if organizing your work and social life around your kids' needs weren't enough of a challenge, you are probably going to discover that very heated and intense emotions will be entering into the picture. These emotions can include yours, your ex-wife's, the children's, and anyone else who might come into your family's life.

Upon setting up separate households, one or both parents may have some rude awakenings around scheduling even something as straight-forward as transportation. Dads frequently discover how much the kids have depended on Mom's taking responsibility for getting them to the right place at the right time. Often, the primary parent keeps all those schedules in his or her head, along with a list of organizations and activities the kids are involved in and the names of teachers, program supervisors, and friends to call in an emergency. Sometimes, the biggest challenge is transferring that list of contacts from one partner's mind to the others.

AREAS TO CONSIDER

The specifics of what you'll have to take under consideration will depend on a variety of factors. It would be rare in a family for just one parent or the other to be doing everything where the kids are concerned, so even though you might think you were handling the bulk of things, rest assured this was probably not the case. Now that you're in your own place, it's very possible that you'll be finding yourself taking on issues that you had completely taken for granted in the past. Don't overlook what may seem like minor issues, such as getting the kids to share the chores, monitoring their behavior at mealtimes, making certain they do their homework, or arranging driving groups.

You might not even know what questions to ask as you learn to take over all of the responsibilities of a home, so I have created a list for you and your ex to review and share. When you were married, were you the one who handled the logistics of who does what, when, and where? Are you the one with the lists and responsibilities in your head? If you were, put yourself in your ex-wife's shoes as you are making the transition.

Recognize that true collaboration begins with making your information about the logistics that involve the kids available to her. If you have a list of other parents or friends who you've depended on to get the kids around to after-school activities, make up a copy of this list for the children's mom. If some of the names require explanation, such as how that person can be helpful or whom you'd only call in a pinch, be sure to write this down. If you find yourself resisting, just put your kids in the foreground of your consciousness and remind yourself that you are doing this to make their life easier.

A Checklist of Responsibilities

- Arrange for babysitters or after-school care.

- Organize after-school activities such as sports, art classes, etc.: this may include getting your kids enrolled, scheduling for days when activities occur, transportation, co-ordination with other parents, and purchasing special clothes or equipment.

- Visits with friends: transportation to and from your kids' friends' houses for visits.

- Special health problems: doctor visits, making certain teachers and babysitters know how to administer medication, and handling any emergencies.

- Shopping and mealtime schedules

- Holiday and summer schedules: what happens when school is out, the kids are home, and you're at work?

- Meetings with teachers, other parents, coaches, etc.

- Illness: who takes care of the kids when they're at home sick and you need to be at work?

- Transportation between parents' homes: this gets more complex depending on the ages of the children and how far apart the parents' homes are geographically.

- Holiday sharing: where the children spend special holidays can often become a point of contention between parents and even between children and parents.

BETWEEN FRIENDS

If resources such as networks with other parents have been working in the past and can be employed again with your new living arrangements, do what you can to keep them working. If your kids are used to specific babysitters, keep them on the call list. This won't always be possible, of course. For example, if you've moved far enough away from the family home that the contacts you had are no longer applicable, obviously those old resources are not going to serve you. But while kids may feel relationships are tenuous at home, keeping the other people they know and love involved will give them stability.

Recognize that some friends and acquaintances may have turned against you because they were more your ex-wife's friend than yours. Don't forget that when we're in the midst of a marital breakup, most of us vent to our friends and almost nobody under the circumstances tells or even sees the whole truth. Some of the people who once helped you and your ex-partner may not feel like extending the same favors they did in the past. Try to keep it in perspective as one of the ways we have of distancing ourselves from a person with whom we have shared an important part of our lives—and whom, in many cases, we still love. Collaborative divorce requires holding a broad perspective of understanding and compassion, not just for our ex, but also for ourselves.

Your support group, including your ex and her friends that love and support your children, is necessary, even if they aren't easy to work with. For your kids' sakes, keeping interactions amicable—collaborative—is the best possible option. The Buddhists teach that "Right Speech" is essential for a satisfying life. The same might be applied to creating and maintaining a collaborative divorce and friendships made while you had been a couple. Right Speech includes precepts such as: *telling the truth, refraining from unjust criticism of others, using language constructively rather than harshly, and refraining from gossip.* Since avoiding the truth, criticizing others, using harsh language, and gossiping are all ways that we vent our pain, frustration, confusion, and anger when a relationship breaks up, honoring the tenets of Right Speech may not be so easy. Without judging yourself or others for violating them, try to keep these tenets in mind, using them as guidelines for successful, collaborative divorce. The more successful your efforts to maintain Right Speech, the more successful you'll be at creating a collaborative relationship with your ex. And that is the right choice for your children.

HOMEWORK, TV, GAMES, & LEISURE

While your children are in your care, you will need to take the time to pay attention to how they are spending their time. That includes observing how many hours they are spending in front of the TV or on social media. What kinds of programming are they being subjected to? What are the video games and CDs they have in their libraries? Watch enough of them yourself so that you can determine the kinds of values and human relationships these entertainments are modeling for your kids.

It may be that your family already has daily routines and screen time limits, and if those are working well for your kids, don't try to reinvent the wheel! However, if you haven't addressed these issues, it is on you to establish house rules that teach good time management.

Look also at the time your children (and you) are spending with their homework and reading—and with you reading to them. The bond established between parents and children reading books together, snuggled up on the couch or in bed, is high-quality time. Not only do they have the experience of reading, but also the closeness of this time together is precious to them.

And what about homework? Even younger children get homework these days. If you have any questions about the kinds and amounts of homework your children are being assigned, check with their teachers. Often, parents ask, "What if I don't have any background in what my child is learning?" Never fear. In most cases, you don't have to know. Tell your child outright that you don't know, and then ask them to teach you. This reversal of roles is one of the best teaching devices around. In explaining things to you, your child is forced to think about what she is learning. Helping you understand will help her understand and will even deepen her appreciation for her own knowledge.

Sometimes, however, you've just got to dig in and find out more about what your child is studying. If you need help, the child's teacher is your best resource. Usually, that means making an after-school appointment with the teacher, so you'll have to schedule it in to your already overly busy days.

When I was writing this section of the book, I asked several teachers I know what advice they would give fathers about how to handle homework responsibilities. All said the same thing: *Set a regular time for homework. Television and internet off. Any activities going on in the house that might be distracting to the student should be suspended. Create an atmosphere conducive to study. If you have letters to write or anything that you may have brought home to do for your own homework, do it during the time your child is studying. Your involvement with your own homework provides an excellent model.*

All of this takes time and patience, as you probably already know. The payoff is not just good grades but children with greater respect for their own knowledge, a sense that self-discipline can bring rewards, and high self-esteem.

THE FAMILY DOG
(AND OTHER CRITTERS)

Your children aren't the only ones you've been responsible for in your old home, your old family. There are often furry children that are also affected by the divorce and establishment of two separate homes. In *The Complete Holistic Dog Book,* authors Jan Allegretti and Katy Somers, D.V.M., point out that dogs develop strong emotional attachments to the families in which they live: "When we bring a domesticated dog into our household, we become his pack, and assume the responsibility of meeting his needs for social interaction and protection." When families break up, our companion animals may become insecure and fearful about what is going to be their fate. And, in fact, they've got good reason to worry. Sometimes, family pets are put up for adoption. All too often, a breakup means that the family pets will be euthanized.

If animals are a part of your family, give thought and discussion to how you will accommodate them in the new order. Will the landlord at your new place even allow animals? Will your ex keep the pet? Will you need to find this valued member of your family a new home? If that's the case, how will the kids handle the fact that their animal friend will no longer be part of the family? Consider the fact that they, too, require time and caring, just as your children do.

Cats are a bit easier to accommodate, mostly because they're content to spend their time alone at home. But each animal has its individualized needs and you'll have to take the time to learn what those are. Your children, of course, depending on their attachment to animal companions, should have a say in all this.

While the fate of animal companions may not be uppermost in your mind at the time of your divorce, do your best to consider their welfare. While you may or may not have been the one to bring them into your family in the first place, someone in your family wanted them and, like it or not, that saddles you with the responsibility of dealing with their fate. Animals need affection and caring, occasional doctor visits, perhaps a nightly walk, and the time and expense of feeding and grooming them.

Most of the time, families do a good job of making certain their animal companions are cared for and that their rights are respected. The bonds we have with animals can be as powerful as the bonds we form with other humans. Not everyone feels this way, of course, but if there are these kinds of deeply felt bonds in your family, give them careful consideration. Your pet parenting will adjust your daily schedule, adding in walks and fetch to your already busy day.

JOINT CUSTODY, JOINT DECISIONS

Joint custody arrangements, while giving the children the opportunity to spend equal time with both parents, also require a high level of collaboration. If the children are splitting their time between your house and their mom's, you'll want to keep communication channels open and clear between you, your ex, and your kids. Some of the issues you'll need to work out are obvious, others not quite so.

While the following list is addressed to people with joint custody arrangements, it will, of course, apply whether you have regular joint custody or only have your kids with you on weekends or a certain number of days or weeks per year:

Open Calendar: You, your ex, and the kids will need to keep joint calendars. This includes not only which days are yours to have the kids, but also what their schedule of activities will be like during the time they're with you. If you're working full time outside of your home, you may need to make arrangements for transportation. Keeping these calendars current and detailed is essential, requiring a high degree of cooperation from everyone, so collaborative skills will be particularly important here.

Clothes and Personal Items: Do the kids keep extra wardrobes at your house, or do they transport everything back and forth? Be sure to get a second set of toiletries and grooming items for your kids, and make sure you stock up on their preferences. Children can be very choosy about this stuff.

Food: Make sure you are clear about the kids' food. You may want to indulge them with their favorite snacks, especially in the initial stages of the new living arrangements, but be aware that if you don't maintain some controls over eating habits in the first place, you may be contributing to a food problem in the future. If you are not familiar with the kids' diets—and many fathers are not unless they were doing both the shopping and cooking prior to the divorce—be sure to sit down decide together what's appropriate to feed them.

Shopping: If you have the kids with you on a regular, scheduled basis, you're most likely going to find yourself shopping with them. If this is a new experience for you, be sure to take the time to figure out a good routine. Kids generally like to go to the supermarket with Mom or Dad, but you'll quickly learn that kids want to act on impulse. There will be lots of excitement, begging for this or that, and crying when you tell them no. Set clear limits from the start, and you will do okay. You'll eventually work out your own routine, in your own style, but for the first few trips to the store with your kids, focus on teaching them good behavior in the store—no nagging, no crying, no running in the aisles. Keep the first shopping trips limited to picking up no more than a dozen items. In that way, you can make the main focus of the trip a learning experience—for you and for the kids!

Allowances: It's a good idea for older kids learn financial responsibility. Having their own money can be a good way to teach them financial responsibility. Coordinate this with your ex rather than giving two separate allowances, one from you and one from their mother.

Holidays: During the big nationally hyped holidays, such as Thanksgiving and Christmas, when there is tremendous pressure

for families to come together, anxieties are always high—even under the best of circumstances. Try to schedule your children's time
with you well in advance—in fact, months in advance. Some parents trade holidays on alternate years. One of the things parents
have to account for, especially as the children get older, is that the
kids, also, will need to have a say in where they go. They may have
plans to spend time with friends who live in one place or another,
and then you've got to choose which is more important: sticking
to the plan or allowing the children to weigh in on the decision.
This collaboration thing doesn't stop with you and your ex; it must
include the kids.

Chores: The idea of assigning roles and responsibilities to
the kids is a good one. Even younger children can "help Dad"
with simple tasks such as picking up toys after playtime or putting yesterday's newspapers into the recycling bin. If you take
care to assign tasks that are age-appropriate, the kids' help really
will ease your daily tasks and also give the child a sense of making a valued contribution.

Bathing: Depending on where you've previously placed your
priorities, you may or may not have been involved in getting the
kids bathed and in bed at night. If you're not familiar with the
bathing routine, check with the kids' mom and get the lowdown.
For younger kids, close supervision is important, requiring a good
chunk of time prior to bedtime.

Laundry: If you have a washing machine and dryer in your
apartment or house, you're in fairly good shape. But if you are
dependent on trips to the laundromat, it's a trip you'll have to
schedule. What do you do with the kids while the Maytag is grind-
ing away? And when do you make time in your busy day for that?
Top priorities when you're looking for your first post-divorce

home should include making sure you have laundry facilities on the premises, if not right inside your abode. After that, you can learn about fabric softener, baby soft detergents, bleach, and spot removers. And, of course, you surely know about washing the whites separately!

Health issues: Who takes the kids to the doctor and dentist? And where do you go when your four-year-old falls down on her tricycle and cuts her lip? If these are unknown destinations for you, organize and record all the necessary information. If you've moved away, use your parenting network for recommendations for pediatric medical and dental providers. And do this before you are faced with an emergency. Most of them are minor, if a bit bloody, but do be prepared by knowing where to get help when you need it. Knowing the route to an urgent care center or hospital can save you a lot of anxiety on that rare (hopefully) occasion when you and your child might need it. As for the routine appointments, they are, in most cases, only a couple times a year. Still, who takes the kids for their annual checkups or their teeth cleanings is something you and your ex will need to work out, and which you may well have to make room for in your life.

GOING FORWARD

I have written this book from the perspective that many fathers will be reading this before a final settlement has been made with their exes. In this way, the book may help you and your ex have more informed expectations and make more informed decisions about how you will share responsibilities and the kinds of time you spend with your children.

Most of what we've discussed in this chapter applies to fathers who have joint custody and whose kids will be spending regular time in their home. But not all fathers, for any number of reasons, have this arrangement. Because of work, the distance you live from your kids, or the fact that you and your ex made a mutual agreement that the kids should not be shuffled back and forth between two homes, the kids might only come to stay with you for a month during their summer vacation or every other weekend. If you're a non-custodial father, much of the above material still applies to you!

No matter what your new routine looks like and how your responsibilities and roles change, you can maintain strong relationships with your kids, still be the greatest dad.

CHAPTER FIVE:

NON-CUSTODIAL PARENTING

"It doesn't matter who my father was;
it matters who I remember he was."
—Anne Sexton

While many states encourage joint custody, with both parents taking equal responsibility and having approximately equal time with the kids, this isn't always possible. For example, one or the other parent may have demands at their jobs that don't allow them to be home as much as the children need them to be. Sometimes, geographic distances prohibit such an arrangement. Think how complicated it would become if the children were with Mom three days a week, Dad for four days a week if

the households were in two different cities! Besides living in two
households with two different sets of standards, if the residences
were in two cities, the kids would have to be enrolled in two different schools and would have two different sets of friends. Faced
with such dilemmas, parents simply have to get together and work
out what is healthiest for the kids. State laws protecting children's
rights usually have pretty carefully drafted regulations to support
what's best for kids. Your attorney, legal aid society, or a counselor
at family services in your own community should be able to advise
you on this.

There are dozens of reasons that custody of the children
might be assigned to one parent rather than the other. They range
from mutual agreement that this would be best for the kids to the
fact that one parent or the other is deemed to be psychologically
unfit or is unable to care for them because of a physical disability,
a mental impairment, or a chronic illness.

In general, it is expected that parents establish a balanced
share of responsibilities. This often means that the non-custodial
parent shall provide whatever financial support they can to make
it possible for the custodial parent to either stay at home, if they're
not working, or provide outside help if they are. Life being what it
is, this balance of responsibilities isn't always possible, as when the
non-custodial parent is, for one reason or another, unemployable.

The experience of being the non-custodial parent has its own
unique challenges, not the least of which is the emotional toll of
being separated from your kids. Even when you have chosen to
be the non-custodial parent, it isn't easy, though understanding
the nature of these challenges can certainly help prepare you for
making the changes necessary. The following story, drawn from
real life, can give you a rough idea of what you'll have to deal with.

A TALE OF TWO CITIES

When Jane and Rob divorced, Rob was in the middle of changing jobs. In fact, the last straw, as Jane saw it, was when Rob unilaterally made the decision about taking the job. While she knew his company was reorganizing and a change might be forthcoming, she had warned him that she would never consider moving. They'd been having trouble in their relationship for two years anyhow, but the crux of her position against moving was that it would mean pulling the kids, Marsh and Tricia, out of school, as well as out of after-school activities they really loved, and asking them to abandon friends they'd grown up with. Rob, however, was just as adamant about the new job since it meant a major career advancement and a 35 percent increase in pay. As an aerospace engineer, this was his dream job, and there was no way he'd turn it down.

From the beginning, Jane and Rob acknowledged the problems they were having in their relationship and had discussed divorcing before the job offer was even on the table. Both had attorneys, so when they got down to drafting their final separation agreements, they had worked out many areas of conflict and were able to come to a relatively amicable settlement. They mutually agreed that if Rob took the job in a city nearly 1,000 miles away, Jane would maintain custody of the children and Rob would provide financial support, making it possible for her to be a full-time, stay-at-home mom. Rob considered Jane a great mom and wanted this stability for his kids. He knew that if he had joint custody, it would mean hiring a live-in nanny for the time the kids were with him. With the children's best interests in mind, he willingly chose to be the non-custodial parent. Being highly motivated in his career, Rob knew joint custody would never work. He would, however, organize his work life so that he could spend short blocks of quality time with his children throughout the year.

Rob may have chosen to be a non-custodial parent, but he had no intention of giving up his rights as Marsh and Tricia's dad. In the agreement he and Jane worked out, Rob would be consulted and would have an equal say about the children's education; any medical issues that might arise; social freedoms and responsibilities, such as dating when they were older; and vacation planning. The latter was particularly important to both parents since it would largely be during vacations that Rob scheduled his time with the kids and Mom would be having a block of time to herself.

While the changes in this family's life went relatively smoothly, Rob soon found that he missed his kids far more than he'd ever imagined he would. He wasn't there the day Marsh had a bad tumble on his bike, requiring several stitches to his forehead. He was enough of a doting father that he called several times a day to see how Marsh was doing, though his ex assured him that his son was doing fine. Nor was he there for the spring pageant in which Tricia played a forest nymph. And then there were the evenings when, after a long day at work, Jane called to get Rob's support with a behavioral problem from one of the kids. Each event in his children's life reminded him that he was no longer participating in their day-to-day life.

Like many fathers who are actively building their professions, businesses, or careers, time at home had always been limited. Rob had often left the office at 8 or 9 in the evening, arriving after the children were already in bed. He missed a lot of what went on in the house during the day. He always heard about victories and conflicts after the fact. From 1,000 miles away, he felt more emotionally distant than ever, of course, and found himself feeling nostalgic about experiences he'd been just as happy to avoid at one point in his life. In some ways, he now participated in the challenges of parenting more than he ever had, though it involved long phone conversations with both his ex and his kids, helping them in whatever way he could to navigate the rougher seas of their lives.

ADVICE FROM A DAD WHO KNOWS THE ROPES

As the non-custodial parent, I certainly missed being a part of my children's daily lives after their mother and I divorced. I had a particularly difficult time around holidays, birthdays, first dates, and my younger son's first confrontations with the panhandlers in the city. Because of even the slight geographic distance separating us, I had to fight against a tendency to drift away emotionally as well. It wasn't intentional—that's for sure—but when I sensed the distance growing or too much time elapsing between phone calls and visits, I began making more conscious and deliberate efforts to stay in touch. Each week, I'd mark days on the calendar when I'd promise myself to call or, during birthdays and holidays, to plan a special get-together. I looked forward to my time with the kids, and I enjoyed thinking about upcoming celebrations, such as birthdays, when I could buy a nice gift for one of my kids or phone with something to share about my own life.

I remember looking for any excuse to send a little gift—a stuffed toy, when my daughter was little, a poster or a CD that I thought one of the kids would like. While these gifts didn't take the place of a father's love and his enjoyment of watching his kids grow up, they were important reminders of the love we shared. All my children have told me, at one time or another, that they looked forward to my regular phone calls and visits. They never doubted I was still very much a part of their lives and that I never stopped caring about them and taking pride in being their dad.

A man in a divorced father group told me how he shared the time apart with his daughter. She was a person who loved to read, a habit she'd learned from her father, who was an English teacher at a community college. They shared the books they were reading, passing them back and forth, trading and sharing what they'd learned from them. They wrote to each other nearly every night, sharing ideas from the books they read and, sometimes, telling how the books taught them something about their own lives. That was a wonderful way for these two to stay in touch, for the literary conversations often spilled over into personal issues they were dealing with.

There were certainly times when I felt depressed, missing my children and wishing I could spend more time with them. Before my ex moved three hours away, I was quite active in their after-school activities and day-to-day lives.

It is the non-custodial parent's job to make up for the distance and lack of time. I needed to encourage myself to go the extra mile and stay connected with my children and also my ex-wife. It's definitely not easy, especially in the early stages when you're still angry and disappointed, but you must do it. Stay in touch however you can, and gracefully let go of any illusions you may have once had about controlling minor issues. Just be sure you're on deck to handle the major issues that come to every child growing up.

THE IMPORTANCE OF
EVERYDAY INFLUENCE

Many single fathers I know worry that without their daily guidance, the kids can easily go astray. They also worry that their kids will lose interest in them or stop loving them, or their kids will think that Dad doesn't love them anymore. Without a father figure at home, will they get in trouble? However, parenting experts and psychologists tell us that it is not the *amount* of time you spend with your kids that counts so much as the *quality* of time you spend with them. If, as the non-custodial parent, you only spend weekends with your children, or perhaps only vacation periods, you are still a very powerful and important influence in their lives. They don't, however, need long lectures from you or heavy-handed guidance. What they need is your attention focused on them in the most loving, caring way you can. That's best expressed by being present with them and listening to them, letting them know that their feelings, what they think about, and their accomplishments and challenges are important to you.

Your children need to feel that they are in your thoughts even when they're not with you physically. Keep tabs via phone, email, video chat, or text, either directly or through their mother. And you can help support their perception that they are present in your thoughts by having evidence of their place in your life posted throughout your home. For example, have photos of them displayed throughout your place. If you have artwork they've done, display it on your walls. If they have given you gifts over the years, make sure those gifts are in evidence when they come to visit. One dad I know tells the story of how his daughter gave him an apron to wear when he was cooking and doing kitchen chores. Across the front were big red letters that said, "My Dad is cookin'!" He hated that apron. It stayed in a kitchen drawer whenever his daughter wasn't there, but when she came to visit, out it came. They even went through a little ritual of her tying it on for him each time he cooked when she came to visit. He wasn't exactly the apron-wearing kind of guy, but this simple ritual sent his daughter a message that she had a permanent place in his life, one that didn't go away when she went home to Mom.

I once visited an architect friend who had divorced his wife when his son, their only child, was four years old. I was always fascinated by how my friend held his little son in his lap while he was working at his drawing board. He always set the boy up with a piece of his own drawing paper, pinned over Dad's drawings. The child contentedly drew pictures on his paper while Dad worked on his. This, to me, was the essence of quality time between a father and his young son. It was no surprise, years later, when the son became a book illustrator and cartoonist. That time together at the drawing board was not only a time of bonding for father and son but apparently got the son in touch with a natural talent that would later be the basis of his career in graphic arts.

How you create quality time together with your children is up to you. You'll find the secret is in choosing something you can do together that you're genuinely interested in, that your kids are interest in, and which you can have fun doing together. If the activity requires physical or mental skill development, always be patient and accept your children's efforts without critiquing every move they make. Do it for the pleasure of sharing this time together and allowing your child to develop their skills at their own pace. Remember, it's the quality of the relationship that counts far more than a finished artifact, or a home run, or a ball well thrown.

Virtual Visitation: Virtual Visitation is the use of electronic communication tools as a means of enhancing parent-to-child communication for non-custodial parents. One of the most important things for children in long distance parenting is consistent and frequent contact. Video chat apps such as Facetime, Skype, and Zoom are excellent tools but must to be used wisely and never as a replacement for physical interactions.

Virtual Visitation is recognized by many states and can be included in non-custodial parenting agreements. While you may feel like it's not necessary at this point, trust me, it's good to know you have those rights if needed in the future. Just be aware that your ex needs to be able to enjoy virtual visits with the kids as well, particularly at times when they are living with you for any extended length of time.

Some of the examples of how video chat may be used include:

- Birthday or holiday celebrations

- Reading or creating child bedtime stories

- Singing and playing music together

- Helping with homework or special projects

- A child showing a bruise or missing teeth, an award, or other special achievement

- Watching sporting events, music or dance recitals, and other events live as they are happening

- Just hanging out as if you were under the same roof.

DIFFERENT VOICES, DIFFERENT HOMES

Keep in mind that one of the reasons you and your kids' mom divorced was that you had slightly, or maybe dramatically, different ways of looking at the world. While it's true that people divorce for a wide variety of reasons, fundamental views of how things should be done is often at the heart of their conflicts. This is an important point because the chances are quite good that with two separate households, the kids will be going back and forth between two worlds that may be quite different. There may be different rules and expectations, aesthetics, physical comforts, and even material goods. Should you work for consistency between your two households? The consensus of opinion from men and women I've talked with is that the solution lies in recognizing and accepting diversity of opinion and lifestyles. Moreover, learning this was important for their kids, since it taught them to be comfortable with other people's differences. While conflicts arose from time to time, the experience of learning to live in two different households was generally found to be beneficial.

One father, who I'll call Gene, tells how his ex-wife remarried a man who had a good deal more money than Gene. Kimball, the new husband, had a huge house in an upscale neighborhood, fancy cars, and even a yacht. Gene, who was a college teacher, had a far more modest lifestyle. When Gene's son Sam was about twelve years old, he started putting his father down, telling him how his stepfather was a lot richer than him. Gene was hurt, of course, and his first reaction was anger. After calming down a bit, he told his son, "You are really lucky to have Kimball as a stepfather. It's great to be able to afford stuff like he has. But I chose to have a different kind of life. I love teaching and working with students, and I wouldn't trade that for anything. You're right, though, I don't have the kind of money Kimball has. College professors just don't make a lot."

After this talk, Sam never mentioned his stepfather's wealth again. The fact is, he settled down a lot, and never again compared his father's lifestyle with his stepfather's. Gene felt that the lesson he wanted to share with other dads was to not take a defensive posture about differences between the two households. Let the child know that you know there are differences and that when you are at Dad's house, you honor Dad's way of doing things. When you're at Mom's, you honor her way. But this is a skill you will have to explain and model.

In order to have things go smoothly and constructively for your kids, you've got to let go of any efforts to impose your lifestyle, values, and desires on your former spouse. This doesn't mean you can't have your way in your home; in fact, you definitely should. Create your own family schedule for dinner, your own rules about homework, television and social media viewing, and social or free time. Keep rules simple and logical, and you'll get a lot less resistance from your kids about following them. This is a natural way for you to build a trusting and whole relationship with your kids. They know where you stand.

Kids being kids, you're likely to get arguments such as, "That's not the way Mom does it." Or, "Jerry [the child's stepfather] lets me use his computer anytime I want." Your answer, always, is to stick with who you are: "That's fine, son. When you're at Mom's house, I want you to mind her and do things the way she likes you to do. But you're here now, and this is the way we do things here." Present your position with no judgment and no comparisons. Ultimately, the best lesson you can teach your children is that there are different ways to do things, and while you don't insist that yours is the only way, it's your way and it's how you would like them to do things with you.

Ask for input from the kids so that they can feel invested in this process. You'll probably be familiar with rules that your children have to follow at their Mom's, so whenever you can reasonably do so, transplant those rules to your house. However, you should only do this if the rules coincide with your way of living. You'll be surprised at how these house rules are pretty universal even when deeper differences exist between you and your ex. Most house rules, after all, are aimed at keeping the place functioning effectively. Aesthetics may also enter the picture, and that's a personal issue. In addition, you might have religious or spiritual rules that you want followed in your home, such as offering a blessing before meals or having evening prayers.

It does frequently happen that the kids' mother is working on a behavioral change at home that she would like you to support when the kids are with you. This could be any number of things, from toilet training to manners at the dinner table to doing homework or practicing a musical instrument. If the kids' mom tells you she'd like you to follow through on that program when they are with you, do everything in your power to support her efforts. Okay, I know, you're still angry and hurt and the last thing you want to do is cooperate with her. Unless you're practicing for sainthood, this isn't going to be easy. Step back for a moment and remind yourself that by collaborating and helping your kids' mother you are ultimately helping your children.

GET FLEXIBLE, GET CONSISTENT

Quality time, as I've mentioned, is often more important than just quantity. However, you do still have to make time for you kids. Some employers are able to give their employees flex time, such as a day a week when they can work from home. As long as the worker produces what is needed when they are at home, companies are willing to honor such arrangements. If you have a flexible work schedule, it usually means that you have the whole day to get a specific amount of work done, but whether you finish at 5 p.m. or at midnight might make little or no difference. That means that you may be able to schedule activities with your children in the middle of the day when you would normally be at your workplace.

As the non-custodial parent, this is a way to get in a little more time with your kids. Besides, you might just make a few extra points with your ex if you can step in to help. Look upon your efforts as feeding the collaborative spirit. Don't forget that there may be times when you want or need cooperation from her. If you've got flex time at work, consider things such as the following that you might do:

- Volunteer for after-school events

- Volunteer to help out in the classroom (some schools encourage this, some don't)

- Taxi the kids to wherever they need to go that day

- Become an assistant coach on an after-school athletic program

- Give extra help with homework

- Do some shopping with the kids for clothes or other
  things they need

Now, while you're working on making the most of your flexibility, be sure that you are also consistent and reliable for your children. When you are first getting used to this non-custodial parent
routine, you might not have the schedule down yet. For example,
you might not know how long it takes to get from work to pick
up the kids on a Friday night when traffic is heavy. As much as
possible, work these things out ahead of time so that you can show
up on time. Even being twenty minutes late can cause anxiety for
your kids and your ex. Thus, you must make this an indelible rule
in your own mind: *Show up when you say you will.* I cannot say that
strongly enough.

Show up when you say you will.

If you say you'll be there at 7 p.m., be there at 7 p.m. Whatever
you do, never call at 6:35 to say you can't make it. The kids count
on you to be there, and they will be hurt if you're not. But of equal
importance, they will take their clues about being reliable from
you. Like it or not, you are a very important role model in their
life. You're the dad. It's stressful enough for them to have parents
living in two different houses. Don't add to their burden by being
a deadbeat dad, the one who makes lots of promises but can't be
counted on to deliver.

Every dad will fall short once or twice. You'll unintentional-
ly promise things and fail to deliver. Despite extenuating circumstances, the look on a child's face will make you feel like crap.
Everyone understands an occasional cancellation, but do not let
it become a recurring one. The cost is the trust of your children.

OVERCOMPENSATING

I suppose there exists in the dark and mysterious recesses of every divorced father's mind some little element of guilt. My experience is that even when everyone agrees that the divorce was exactly the thing to do, we can still feel regrets for our kids and wish that we'd had the power to make their lives a little easier. While there's nothing terribly wrong about feeling a little guilt and regret, it can lead to actions that can send the wrong signal to our kids. The most likely reaction on our part is to try to make up for what we regret—in short, to overcompensate.

The take-home message is to realize that what your kids want from you is not stuffed toys or video games and CDs, but your presence and your caring in their lives. Deliver this, and you won't slip into being a guilt-ridden dad who doesn't show up when he needs to. And you won't be tempted to compensate with material presents, either. You'll know and value yourself and be open to giving of yourself and enjoying your time with your kids. While you might be feeling guilty or remorseful for blowing it on rare occasions—and I want to emphasize the word "rare"—or you might feel guilty for having the marriage fail, but it is important to *not* shower the kids with gifts, money, or too much freedom. Believe me, it won't work in the long run.

Your kids' top priority is that they need you as a father. Toys, vacations, and parties on the occasional weekend may be okay, but not if you are giving those things because you're feeling too guilty to give of yourself. Your kids need you to be present on a regular basis, as a caring, accountable, and responsible father. This is the best gift you can ever give your kids, and it is a gift that will be cherished all their lives. It is also a gift that you are giving to yourself. It may take a while to settle down immediately after the divorce, but when it does, there will be no gift more valuable than Dad's attention and love.

HANG IN THERE

It takes time to adjust to being the non-custodial parent, particularly if you're accustomed to seeing your kids every day. For a long time, your life can feel very empty, though in some ways, life can also seem simpler. Not much to do when you get home at night! But without the kids in your daily life, you can get a bit lonely or even depressed. As one man put it, "For months, I felt shipwrecked. Every night after work, I returned to my empty apartment and felt like I'd just landed on a desert island."

It's tempting to look for ways to fill the void. Some men do it by jumping back into dating, looking for a new job, or taking up a new sport or hobby. It can feel like it would be easier to not see your kids at all, to move to another state so that the wounds of separation weren't reopened every week or two after a visit from the kids. A new girlfriend, a new job, moving to another city, finding new friends and new activities that will keep you from thinking too much about your life can all bring some instant relief; this is true. Trouble is, in most cases, men start thinking about their kids again. You can't escape the reality that they are out there and they want you to be in their lives.

What works during the early stages of discovering yourself as a non-custodial dad? I'll tell you, if you want to get this thing working for you and the kids as quickly as possible, get some help. This could be a friend who has made the leap across the gap and is presently pretty happy with the arrangement he's developed with his kids. It could be a pastoral counselor who is able to help you process some of your feelings and help you get more focused and clear about them. Or it could be a psychotherapist. If you haven't done any inner work, exploring who you are and what you're about, now's the time.

This is the time to swallow your pride and hurt feelings, do some process work on your anger, and stay put. Do not leave town. The kids need their dad, and dad needs the kids. So, relax, take a deep breath or two, and use this time as an opportunity for personal growth. You're well on your way to maintaining that coveted title: World's Greatest Dad.

CHAPTER SIX:

SETTLING LEGAL AND CUSTODY ISSUES

"Because of great love, one is courageous."
—*Lao Tzu*

The day you consult with an attorney, or set your divorce proceedings into motion within the legal system, a whole different relationship begins to evolve with your soon-to-be-ex. Negative feelings and arguments you and your partner have been struggling with privately are now being discussed with a stranger, sometimes who have a particularly adversarial way of negotiating. However, in recent years, many attorneys have taken a different approach, particularly in family law, and especially where children are involved. Nevertheless, it's important to note that as you move from your conflicts with your wife having been more or less private, to the more public expression of your conflict through lawyers and the court, something quite different can evolve in your relationship.

You may lie awake nights asking yourself, "How could our relationship have possibly come to this?" You remember how you were once deeply in love with this woman you're now divorcing, and she was deeply in love with you. Maybe there was a time when you both fantasized that your relationship was different from all the rest, that your marriage was special, something that could never be torn apart. You would be together, dedicated to one another for eternity. And now? Well, tighten your seat belts, the ride is turning savage. The center of your relationship has become a skirmish over money, control, and visitation rights.

At this point, there is a single piece of advice I'd hope that every divorcing father would take in and set as an inviolable law: *Do everything you can to avoid hurting the kids. And never forget that if you hurt their mom, you're probably going to be hurting them.* Not easy advice to follow.

There's a wonderful quote that might help you remember what to do now. It's by the author Virginia Burden Tower. She points out that a collaborative relationship, one of cooperation rather than combat, begins with "a thorough conviction that nobody can get there unless everybody gets there."

It's important to be very clear and resolute in setting your intention. This doesn't mean being stubborn or inflexible, but it certainly means holding your own and letting your attorney and your ex-to-be know what you are about. Move through the legal process that's unfolding with the goal of conserving your funds, maintaining your dignity, and minimizing damage to your kids. Remember the old clichés, if nothing else: "Money can't buy happiness." And, "When you go to court, the only sure winners are the attorneys."

As you read the rest of this chapter, keep in mind that what I offer here is not intended as a substitute for expert legal advice. I'm not an attorney, nor do I know how all that I have to offer will translate into the legal framework of your particular situation or the laws of the state where you live. What I do offer is in the realm of handling the new relationship, which is now evolving between you and the mother of your children. I offer what I do with the assumption that you are getting legal counsel and if any questions are raised here that will enter into the legal process, you will discuss them with your attorney.

ENDING THE WAR

When we're angry, hurt, and our financial coffers are under siege, let's face it, most guys declare war. Maybe it's in the genes, I don't know. And if you think it's just a guy thing, think again. Under fire, women are easily as warring as us men; they just have somewhat different tactics and somewhat different weapons. Let me warn you, if you maintain a warring attitude while trying to settle the legal affairs of your divorce, it's going to cost you. And it'll cost you big. So, before you put on your armor and drag your weapons into the courtroom, let's review the rules of collaboration and compassionate engagement. From the outset, you'll be seeking an outcome that, to paraphrase Virginia Burden Tower, is based on a conviction that *nobody gets there unless everybody gets there.* Is this always going to be possible? No. But you need to do everything you can to hold that intention until it's clear that she's thrown down the gauntlet and you have no choice but to pick it up.

In every human interaction, you can count on one of three outcomes: 1) you're going benefit from the interaction, 2) nothing much will be happening at all, or 3) you'll come out the worse for it. There will be many interactions ahead, lots of them tense, and it is how you choose your arsenal that will determine whether you, and your kids, come off better for it.

It is unrealistic to hope for a win-win situation after you've filed for divorce; you're both hurt, the attorneys are fighting for what they think is in their client's best interest, and the kids are being pulled between two struggling people whom they love. Finances are tight, your new living situation is tight, and emotions are tight. But even though having a perfectly amicable divorced relationship is unrealistic, you still have to try, if only to protect your kids.

Your primary concern must be to develop a co-parenting plan that is the best for your children. This is big stuff, and now, it's time to embrace the collaborative process.

COLLABORATION IS THE KEY

What's the bottom line? By far, your best strategy is to avoid creating a contentious and hostile situation as you work out your divorce settlement. A badly handled divorce inevitably turns into a never-ending source of distrust, despair, and anger. The legal phase of divorce is a time to tread lightly if at all possible. Being someone who is easy-going will serve you well in your effort to end the war or, at least, call a truce.

I am not saying to raise the white flag and surrender to an unfair settlement since this will likely make you increasingly resentful and angry. Instead, chill out and calmly take control. If you should be backed into a situation where a vigorous legal battle is absolutely necessary, be well prepared; just recognize that there's little to gain and a great deal to lose if you get mean. Remember, the people who are going to be hurt aren't just you and your ex; it's your children. You have at least some choice in this matter; the kids don't.

Collaborating could look like using some of the lists contained in this book to help you determine what your priorities are. Take that list of priorities to your ex (or her lawyer) that outline how you see joint custody or visitation, finances, transportation, etc., working after you've moved into your own place. It could be that collaboration is agreeing to abide by rules of civility and discussing legal representation. However you decide to work it out, be determined to act in a spirit of collaboration, even when anger fuels the flames.

CREATE A PAPER TRAIL

"Divorce is the one human tragedy that reduces everything to cash."
—*Rita Mae Brown*

My advice is to stay out of court for the good of your kids, your self-esteem, and your pocketbook. But if it comes to that, do all you can to protect yourself. You can be attacked whether you expect it or not, and a few good habits will prevent a world of legal sorrow.

The legal system operates on allegations and verifiable evidence. From your side of the fence, make it a rule to never level allegations against your ex unless the situation absolutely ethically demands it or your children would be victims if you didn't; be sure that you are not fooling yourself about your ethics. These situations do exist, however. Be sure to get good legal advice if you have evidence of child abuse or neglect. If you have good cause to believe that there is a problem with addiction or illegal activities, seek legal advice, collect evidence that will hold up in court, and be ready to stand your ground.

It's distressingly common for one party in a divorce to opportunistically spin a minor human foible into a serious moral issue. For example, a man I'll call Richard accused his ex to be psychotic and unfit to have custody of their only child, Carinna, who was sixteen years old at the time. The only evidence Richard could offer was that his ex raged at him whenever he showed up at her doorstep and that she had been like this for years during their marriage. While it was true that Richard's ex raged at him, she was anything but psychotic. She held down a respectable job and people at work liked her, and an investigation by social services indicated that she was an excellent mother. Richard may have been telling the truth that his ex-wife raged at him, but his allegations that she was psychotic were way off base. She might have had a temper, but psychotic she was not. In court, his allegations cost him his credibility, and his ex ended up the winner.

There's a lesson for us all in Richard's story. Often, when we're particularly angry and hurt, a relatively minor foible in the other person can seem like reason to keep the kids away from your ex. We could even say that there are times when our ex's behavior toward us can seem over the top or just plain nuts. But make sure you know what you are talking about and can provide evidence of your allegations before you open your mouth. Don't fool yourself and hurt the kids in the process.

How can you make the strongest showing in court? Instead of attacking, spend your time and energy showing that you're professional in your dealings with others; that is, that you're reasonable and you exercise the highest ethics. You don't make points by alleging the moral decay of others.

When you get even a hint that you might be heading for the divorce court, do everything you can to prepare for it. That preparation begins with documentation. Wherever possible, create a paper trail. Organize receipts of expenses for the kids. Keep a journal with dates, times, and outlines of discussions you have had with your ex or your attorneys. Take the time to write down telephone calls you make to your ex, and calls she makes to you. If you both have email, keep an electronic file of your communication in a file that you can later print out. If you make an oral agreement by phone or in person, back it up with an email to her. Say in the email that you want to confirm with her that such and such was your agreement. This can be helpful for everything from making dates to pick up the kids to tentative agreements as earthshaking as who gets custody of the goldfish.

If you and your ex are active emailers, use it to document implied consent, such as changing plans regarding the children while they are with you. Through the email, explain your situation in adequate detail, and with plenty of advance time to get a reply. Tell her what you intend to do and add a phrase such as, "Let me know if there are any problems with this." She can answer with an objection, which then needs to be addressed. If you don't get an answer of any kind back from her, it could mean either that she is ignoring you or she hasn't checked her email. A follow-up phone call is then in the offing. In the meantime, you've got a copy of your email to document your request.

One caution about email: While it's a good way to make and confirm appointments, or to cross reference an agreement you have made, or are in the process of making, don't try to deal with emotional issues this way.

Don't carry this business of documenting everything to extremes. For example, I've seen people run around with little recorders in their pockets, insisting that every conversation with their ex get taped. If you want your relationship to get really tense, I guarantee this will do the trick.

HOW WILL YOU PROCEED?

There are different ways that you can move forward with divorce proceedings, and here is a brief overview of your options.

Do-It-Yourself Divorce: Thousands of couples each year handle their own divorces. If your case is simple, neither of you is contesting the divorce, and both of you have been able to work out agreements and terms, then do-it-yourself divorce can be a good option. It'll save both of you the expense of an attorney. In most cases, self-help divorce has got to be a collaborative effort. There are several books and software packages now available to guide you through this process.

How do you know if a do-it-yourself divorce will work for you? You'll both want to ask that question, and answer it honestly before proceeding. Here are some guidelines to help you with this decision:

- Are you able to sit down and fairly work out your issues together?

- Do you have few assets to divide up and are you in agreement about how to share them?

- Do both you and your spouse have a steady source of income?

- Are neither of you contesting the divorce?

- Do you have the time and ability to handle the necessary paperwork?

Therapy for Developing Agreements: If you're getting stuck with your divorce agreements but still feel you can work things out with a little help, consider finding a therapist who is willing to help you sort out the basic financial and custody issues agreements. Therapists are usually considerably less expensive than lawyers and they offer the *added value* of helping you process and heal some of the anger you and your ex are carrying. This is a good alternative if you are involved in an uncontested divorce, but it will work only if you and your spouse are in a place where you can agree to cooperate.

Before your first session with such a therapist, be sure you and your ex are clear about the points you need to cover, though you may not be in full agreement about dollar amounts and specific custody arrangements. Not every therapist will be willing to work with you, so you'll want to make certain you tell anyone you're interviewing exactly what you want from them. For example, you might wish to tell a therapist you are considering that you'd like them to help you and your ex sort out the emotional from the practical issues, which may make coming to an agreement much easier. Tell this person that you and your ex are doing your best to handle the divorce collaboratively and let him or her know how you're doing with this so far.

When you've done all that you can with your therapist, take the results to your respective attorneys to fine-tune and process or, if you are working on a do-it-yourself divorce, you can simply move forward with your filing.

How to Use a Mediator: You can also consider hiring the services of a mediator to help you work out a divorce settlement. While mediators are trained in the law, they are usually not lawyers. Instead, their expertise is in helping people work through their legal problems outside the courts. You might say they are trained to coach you through the process to an agreement you can both live with. As a third and neutral party, the mediator moderates communications between you and your ex as it pertains only to forging the legal document proclaiming you divorced.

The mediator's job focuses on helping you create an equitable compromise that will fairly address present and future problems each spouse is likely to face. In mediation, you do not fight; you discuss, listen, and seek compromise. You must stay open and calm as the mediator leads each of your through your various issues and how the courts will view your arguments. Mediators will not tell you what to do, but help you both come to an agreement.

Bring your collaborative stance to mediation and you'll save a great deal of money and pain. Give it your best try. The more you can do to build the collaborative spirit into that new relationship, the more functional, happy, and healthy your extended family is going to be.

Arbitrate This: Similar to mediation, arbitration will be faster, cheaper, and less hassle than the regular attorney-driven divorce process. In arbitration, your attorneys bring the case to the arbitrator who, based upon all the facts on hand, will make a firm decision about your case. Arbitration, unlike mediation, is a binding agreement between you and your spouse and is a very good option if either party is going to flip out later and try to appeal the decision.

The Collaborative Approach: Collaborative divorce is a process through which the parties and their individual attorneys commit themselves to resolving all issues of the divorce by negotiated agreement without resorting, or threatening to resort, to costly court proceedings. Collaborative divorce uses informal methods such as open and voluntary disclosure of financial documents, four-way conferences (spouse and attorney on both sides), negotiation, and, where needed, outside professionals such as accountants, financial planners, and family counselors. While some attorneys may refer to themselves as being *collaborative in style*, fully collaborative law requires commitment to a "no court" policy.

HOW TO CHOOSE AN ATTORNEY

There's a saying in legal circles that sometimes having a good lawyer on your side is more important than having justice on your side. That's a little cynical, but it suggests that sometimes the law is more about who's got the best lawyer than who's in the right. In any case, armed with this realization, you should be alerted to the importance of having a good attorney. A good attorney, like a good doctor, is best searched out through personal and professional referrals. Divorce is not uncommon these days, so your friends, family, therapist, or colleagues will probably have leads

and recommendations for you. If you cannot get any good personal referrals, you can visit or call the

- State bar association

- Legal aid society

- Public defender's office

- Public library lawyer's directory

Just as you might do to select your personal doctor, it's wise to
visit a few attorneys and find the right fit for you. It is appropriate
to ask your prospective attorney for a few referrals to others in
his or her profession. The attorney is going to be the team leader
for your divorce, so get the best one you can, and make sure you
discuss how important it is to not hurt the kids by being overly
aggressive or caustic with their mother.

What to Look for in a Good Attorney: As you begin your
search, I recommend being proactive. Interview your attorney as
if you were interviewing a new employee for a business you are
running. In effect, an attorney is going to be your employee, and
you need to have a pretty good idea of who you're dealing with.
Don't be afraid to ask questions. To guide you in your interview of
her or him, here are some suggestions:

- Ask how many years of successful experience in divorce
  cases they have under their belt

- Ask them to explain any new laws that might affect your
  case. You'll be able to judge from their answer whether
  or not they are keeping up with changes in the laws
  pertaining to divorce cases.

- Let them know that you expect to be informed immediately if any new problems or changes arise in your case.

- Ask them what their policy is on client-attorney confidentiality, and make it clear that you do not want information about you shared with anyone else except by first getting your expressed permission.

- Tell them how important it is to you that they regularly communicate with you and that it will be easy for you to reach them when you need to.

- Tell them that since they will be representing you, it is important that they know your standards: you demand high ethical standards, honesty, quick thinking, and that they have a good relationship with you and the local court officials. Be sure to explain that you are most concerned that your children are not hurt by any legal skirmishes that might arise and that your highest goal is that the relationship with your ex be collaborative rather than adversarial wherever this is possible.

If you are able to bring up these issues in your early interviews, you'll more than likely be able to get a pretty good picture of what your potential attorney is about. If they stumble around or hem and haw around the answers, forget it and move onto the next interview. These questions are designed to elicit responses that will give you plenty of substance to chew on and make your final choice.

GUIDELINES AND FORMULAS
FOR DECISIONS

There are pretty clear state and county guidelines and formulas regarding child support, alimony, and property settlements. With a bit of research, you can get a ballpark idea of what these agencies consider fair and equitable. While these guidelines can cause us all a huge amount of stress, they were established in order to guard the well-being of the children. What you need to know is that the courts will be looking at any settlement from what these guidelines recommend. The courts will follow whatever statutes or other local direction is available.

The standard guidelines for child support in each area may not always seem fair to each individual. But so far, no one has come up with a more satisfactory way of establishing child support payments that works. Somehow or other, you've got to bite the bullet and pay what the courts say. If you can't handle the payments on your present income, you'll need to figure out a way to make up the shortfall, perhaps with a second job or looking for something that pays better. Some men have a tendency to blame their ex for the size of the payments, but if you're feeling like that, keep in mind that it's just the way our society has determined how the pie gets sliced.

The Judge's Rule of Thumb: In cases where divorcing spouses are contesting custody, judges are going to consider your track record with the kids. Have you been a caring, accountable, and responsible parent? You will need to be able to document your past and present track record of taking care of the kids and contributing to their well-being both financially and emotionally. From day one, if possible, you should have the kids live with you at least half the time while you're sorting out the custody agreement. If you only see the kids on occasional weekends and then you go to court demanding joint custody, don't be surprised if you wind up with a limited visitation arrangement.

"What you see is what you get," one father said. "Unless there are well-documented, extenuating circumstances, such as being able to give concrete proof that the kids are better off with you, regardless of the fact that you have not been seeing them every week, the custody arrangement you presently have is the one most judges are going to support."

Conrad was facing extenuating circumstances with his ex-wife, Judy. She had suffered from depression much of her adult life, and when Conrad filed for divorce, she became despondent. At first, she clung to Penny, their child, saying she needed the security of at least knowing that her child would be with her. Wanting to do what was best for everyone, Conrad went along with this and did not immediately press for joint custody. In fact, at his ex-wife's request, he only visited Penny once a week.

The arrangement did not go well. Judy's episodes of depression became increasingly debilitating. She sometimes overlooked Penny's well-being, failing to get her off to school in the morning, and occasionally neglecting her own and the child's nutrition. Penny, who was six at this time, was also developing signs of depression, perhaps mimicking her mother's behavior.

During this time, Conrad was renting the other half of his parents' duplex and thus, had built-in babysitters with his retired parents right next door. He began arguing that the child would be better off in his custody while Judy got back on her feet and was in better condition to care for Penny. Everyone, even Judy's own parents, became concerned. Finally, Conrad went to social services and managed to get the court order changed so that he had full custody of Penny.

Judy was able to make the strides to recover her own health. Today, she and Conrad share custody of Penny and enjoy a genuinely collaborative relationship.

While this is an unusual case, it does point out the complex problems divorcing couples can sometimes encounter. Through genuine concern for the long-term effects on the child of having to live with severe challenges such as I've described here, it is sometimes possible to work out a collaborative approach that works to everyone's benefit.

CUSTODY ISSUES

This is big stuff. When you separate or divorce, your primary concern will be to develop a co-parenting plan that is in the best for the children. This is the time to embrace the collaborative process. If both parents are responsible, loving people who are equally concerned that their children get what's best for them, joint custody is probably going to be the best arrangement you can put together. But, of course, if there is evidence of abuse, violence, or criminal behavior, all bets are off.

Barry, who was a child welfare worker in a mid-western city for many years, stated that "in most cases, joint custody is an excellent solution. It sends as positive a message as possible to the kids, given the circumstances. By that, I mean the kids feel that they are wanted and loved by both parents, and they have regular contact with both of them.

"When I was working with families, I always made a point of telling both parents that the most vital issue we needed to focus our attention on was how we were going to work together to create for the kids a situation where they had free and open access between both parents. We needed to create as normal and fulfilling a life as possible for them. This meant looking at all the different options and models of creating extended families that were open to us."

These are the terms and arrangements that you should be familiar with as you enter into discussions of custody.

Legal Custody: Legal custody means a parent has legal authority to care for and make legal decisions concerning the children's health, education, and welfare. Legal custody is either "joint" or "sole." Unless there is a compelling reason to keep one parent from involvement in decisions, most courts grant joint legal custody even if one parent spends much more time with the children than the other. It means that both parents share equally in decisions that affect the kids even though one parent might only see them occasionally. Generally, courts give sole legal custody to just one parent only if the other parent is completely irresponsible and unfit to participate in decision making together, or if one parent is out of the picture.

Physical Custody: Physical custody refers to living with the children and seeing to it that their day-to-day physical needs are taken care off—feeding them, making sure they are clothed, and getting them to school on time. If you have the children with you only on weekends, on those days you have physical custody; on the other days of the week your ex has physical custody, while the other parent has "visitation" rights. The difference depends more on the state laws and customs of local courts than on the percentages of time.

Split Custody—Separating Siblings: In most families, siblings stay together after divorce, often giving each other crucial stability and support—but sometimes, it's appropriate to make different custody arrangements for different siblings. For example, if one parent plans to move to another city where's there's a great school system that would benefit a younger child, but the older sibling is in her last year of high school, is involved in lots of activities, and wants to stay, the parents might decide to have her live with the parent who's remaining in the original city and send the other sibling with the parent who's moving.

Non-custodial: The prospect of being the non-custodial parent shouldn't be looked at as a negative thing. You can be just as involved in your child's life as the custodial parent, and bear an equal share in the responsibilities of parenthood. It does not mean you're uncaring, unfit, or not present. It certainly doesn't have to define how your relationship with your child should or will be. In most cases, the non-custodial parent is given visitation with their child and the custodial parent must comply with the order.

NEVER CLIMB OUT ON A LIMB WHEN YOUR EX IS HOLDING A SAW

Here's the deal. Divorces are highly emotional and contentious, especially if they get into court—which few do in most states, by the way. Along the way, you are probably going to lose your cool and get just as nasty as anyone else. This will instigate the adversarial atmosphere that every divorcing couple dreads. Unfortunately, it is not unusual for fathers to be attacked in hostile custody fights. When and if you do, invoke the 24-Hour Rule. Don't respond directly to any attacks for at least twenty-four hours.

If you've got a real battle going on, understand that you could be accused of any number of serious wrongdoings, including all types of neglect and abuse. You can immediately vent to your attorney and keep the record straight, should your ex unjustly attack you. Whether you or your ex have initiated a contentious situation, it's wise to stay out of direct contact with her. Don't get pissed off and strike back. The judges do not look favorably upon a dad who gets into an argument, particularly in front of the judge. But it will look good for you if you stay calm in the face of an attack. A good demonstration of grace under fire will position you as a stable family leader. This holds true both in and out of the courtroom.

However, it's very important to set the record straight when accused of something serious. If an accusation is true, sometimes the best tactic is to agree gracefully that you recognize your actions were less than ideal and move on. If it's not true, then calmly present evidence to refute it. Just state your case and move on. If you can anticipate any potentially harmful allegations your ex might bring against you, talk to your attorney about them so that you can develop a good defense.

And, for sure, if there is anything your attorney should know about you before you go to court, put it all on the table with him or her. If you have engaged in any activities that are likely to be used against you, go out of your way to inform him or her of any area of your life that might make you vulnerable. There's nothing worse than having something come out in court that you haven't told your attorney about. Attorneys hate to be caught unprepared. It makes them look bad, and it's inevitably going to hurt you, usually in the form of more restricted visitation or custody rights, higher support payments, and probably a bigger bill from the attorneys. Be honorable and truthful.

DON'T BE A JERK

Coming to a financial settlement when you're wounded and angry is most likely going to put you out there on the edge between
reason and sanity. As Irving, from one of the men's groups confessed, "If I were a bull, I'd have gone on a rampage. It made me
crazy sitting there in court and hearing what was coming down. I
just heard a big sucking sound and knew my financial future was
getting flushed out to sea. Sure, I saw red. And I wanted revenge
at that moment. But my sister had been coaching me for several
weeks, reminding me that I might have to accept that I was going
to be the sacrificial lamb in all this. But she reminded me; I really
do love my kids and want the best for them. And once upon a time,
I loved Lori, too, or those kids wouldn't have ever come into this
world. My sister kept telling me, 'don't forget Lori is the mother
of your children, Irv. Be cool! Be patient. Give it space.' I'm glad I
took her advice. It took a while, but Lori and I are okay with each
other now. Not friends exactly, but not enemies, either."

Your ex might do some pretty outrageous things to you as she
makes an effort to vent all her feelings. But no matter what she says
or does, remember that you are responsible for your own actions.
You may get needled and needled and needled until you want to
lash out or counter-attack. But if you do, you will pay for it dearly.
Do not fall into that trap. Don't be a jerk in the heat of the moment. That could mean practicing superhuman restraint.

Allow me to be perfectly clear concerning the consequences
of losing your restraint. When Mom and Dad get into big battles
in front of the kids, or if you get so out of control that you resort
to physical threats, you can end up with a restraining order against
you, preventing you from going anywhere near your children or

your ex. You may be pretty cool headed most of the time, but I've had two acquaintances I consider to be very sane and reasonable men really go over the edge during divorce negotiations. They both ended up enrolling in anger management classes, giving proof to the courts that it was safe to lift the restraining orders their exes filed against them. Why am I telling you this? Because many of us don't know how to best monitor our own stress levels. We fool ourselves into believing we're on top of things. And then, the heat suddenly goes up a mere two degrees and we lose it.

If you feel you're on the edge of losing that last bit of reason you've been clinging to, do something before you blow up. If you're having trouble with anger, look around for a good anger management class. Talk it over with a good therapist, remembering always that therapists are cheaper than lawyers and the long-term gains of spending a few hours with a therapist can be golden. Sometimes, in the midst of the battle, the very best you can do is invoke the 24-Hour Rule. Withdraw from the battle in order to regroup, which means settling down emotionally and reclaiming some semblance of reason. And this includes holding strong to your ultimate goal of being as collaborative as you can possibly be—*regardless of your ex's actions.*

In most cases, compromises will be necessary. Biting your tongue will be necessary. Count on it. And remember, the compromise that's possible might mean assessing what is the highest good *possible* at this time for your kids. And it could turn out to be true that the *as-good-as-you-can-get* settlement may be far from comfortable for you.

Put yourself in your ex's shoes whenever you can, even if it's just for the moment. That doesn't mean agreeing with her. It only means allowing yourself to take a few moments to grasp, at some very basic human level, that she is fighting from a place she believes in. No, it may not be just and fair by your book. It may not be reasonable. It may even be vindictive, selfish, or just plain nuts by your way of thinking. But by having some feeling for what her experience is about, you'll be better able to hold your own position, acting in a way that won't get you in trouble and that may ultimately work very much in the favor of you and the kids.

You needn't beat the enemy to the ground to win. In fact, if you look at human history, you'll find that lasting peace is never gained that way. It's gained by tenaciously negotiating in good faith. It helps to have the patience of Job, of course, to keep going forward in search of a settlement. Often, that place of peace is beyond your ability to even imagine at the time. It may even come a year or two or three down the line. That's a difficult perspective to keep in mind but if you can, it will make things much easier, and may well be the one thing that keeps you and your kids out of a prolonged court battle.

Just be cautious in swinging too far in the other direction. While not being a jerk, you also needn't be a doormat, giving in to all of her demands without a fight. Collaboration doesn't mean being a "nice guy" and giving away everything you've got. It isn't *peace at any cost.* Your peace must include being there for the kids, and those emotional and spiritual resources need to be honored as much as you honor your bank account.

DEADBEAT DADS

The so-called *deadbeat dad* is all about money and abandoning your kids. Financial problems can be terribly debilitating, no doubt about it. And when things get too tough, and emotional pressures build up, sometimes, it can feel like there's no alternative but to flake out, flee the scene, and abandon your commitment—and that means abandoning your kids. Even in the best of times, we might have financial difficulties. If this is the case and you cannot make your support payments, don't wait until the last minute to contact your ex and let her know what's up. Give her plenty of notice because she is, after all, counting on having the money. If you're in an adversarial relationship with her, you might need to notify your attorney, who can relay this info to her lawyer, and at least be on record for attempting to handle the crisis in a reasonable manner.

If, indeed, you have the money and you're just being a jerk and withholding it, get over it. I'll make no bones about it; that's the worst kind of deadbeat dad.

Adolpho was a freelance journalist who got a divorce at a time when he was riding high, with a syndicated column and lots of speaking engagements that paid excellent money. His divorce settlement took a big bite from his total income, but his income was six figures at the time. Four years later, he lost his syndication and his income dropped precipitously. For two years, he lived on credit, had to sell his house, and got down to where he had only enough money to pay his basic expenses and the interest on his own loans.

With Adolpho's daughter Jeda in college, his ex-wife was getting nuts trying to meet expenses. One day, Adolpho called up his daughter and invited her over to his apartment for dinner, explaining to her that he didn't have money to take her out to a restaurant. He explained the financial situation, informing her that she'd need to take a more active hand in her own support. Though it took some time to come to terms with the shift in responsibility, Adolpho and

Jeda were able to find a solution that didn't include Adolpho with-drawing from his daughter's life or shirking his responsibilities.

By the time Alolpho got his own situation back together; his daughter was well on her way to a successful career path for her-self. No deadbeats here!

OPPORTUNITIES FOR PERSONAL GROWTH

Okay, we've all heard that old homily about every challenge in life being seen as a lesson in our personal evolvement. And by now, you probably feel that you've completed your graduate work several times over and deserve at least your honorary Ph.D. at the University of Hard Knocks. And I'd probably agree with you if I knew what you've been through. I know that I've felt that way more times than I can count, so I won't burden you with my own story. As I look back on those long years of travail during my di-vorce, I have to admit that I learned a lot about patience, negoti-ation, seeking the highest good, and working toward collaborative solutions than I ever would have learned elsewhere, if at all.

Could I have said it was all for the good at the time it was hap-pening? Well, no. So, I probably shouldn't be trying to convince you of the same right now. Nevertheless, take it from someone who's been there and come back with whatever treasure was to be found. Over time, wounds from this period have mostly healed. And, believe me, there were some pretty big ones! Am I grateful for what I had to go through to learn what I did? Well, I'll be honest. I wouldn't go so far as to claim such a thing. But I will say that I'm at peace with myself about those years and, however the lessons came, it's great to have the skills and the wisdom that this difficult time afforded me.

Going through the divorce wars is not one of those "opportunities" you go out looking for. But there's no denying that you're going to face major challenges that will force you to develop strengths and abilities you probably never dreamed were within you. Learning to swim with alligators and sharks may not have been your dream in life, but having done so, and survived, you'll carry a knowledge of yourself that will serve you in limitless ways.

Maybe collaboration is ultimately about this anyway—of holding a mental picture of something greater than the battle of the moment, and holding with your own inner strength regardless of the apparent difficulties!

CHAPTER SEVEN:

GET REAL ABOUT
THE KIDS

*"If you bungle raising your children I don't think
whatever else you do matters very much."*
—*Jacqueline Kennedy Onassis*

I think it's fair to assume that if you have read this far and have
been working to create the collaborative spirit in your divorce,
you already place your children's happiness and well-being high
on your priority list. And that's a big part of the challenge right
there; genuine caring is at least half of good parenting. Your focus on giving your children affection and protection can help to
build emotional security, while guidance that is age-appropriate
and caring can teach self-discipline, the long-term benefits of

cooperation, and a balanced sense of responsibility. These are all healthy habits of living.

As a parent, there will be times when you make mistakes and say things you later regret. And being a divorced parent, you'll probably carry around some guilt about your marriage breaking up, along with worry about what it might do to the kids. Regrets are just part of living, and, sometimes, it seems that having children multiplies our potential for mistakes. As Pete, a single father with the custody of his three children once stated, "If my kids got a nickel for every regretful thing I ever did raising my three boys, they'd be millionaires. Fortunately for me, they have short memories about all that, and they think they've got the best dad in the world. Well, maybe *next best*. On that count, at least, I try not to dash their illusions."

One of the keys of good parenting is knowing what is age-appropriate. When is your growing child ready to learn difficult, coordinated physical activities? For example, catching a ball thrown to him or riding a bicycle? Many of the things we'd like our children to learn when they are young require a specific level of maturity in their neuromuscular development. If you push them to learn things that require physical and mental capacities they have not yet developed, they can end up feeling frustrated and incompetent, as they'll be unable to accomplish what you're asking them to do.

Raising competent, skillful, and self-confident kids starts with knowing when a child's body and mind are developed enough to take on a particular challenge. The younger your child at the time of your divorce, the more important it is to know what is age-appropriate. How will you handle visitation when your child is still nursing—and what will their first diet be like soon after they are weaned? If you are going to have joint custody and your child is a toddler and not yet toilet trained, what will be your responsibilities there? Will you commit to toilet training? Are you up for that? And when would it be appropriate to start your youngster reading?

If you have older children, do you know how to talk with your daughter who is entering puberty and is on the verge of experiencing her first *moon*? And what about your teenaged son's budding interest in sex?

It's amazing how many issues come up with growing children that you may have never given too much thought. Most men begin to discover about this time that they left a lot of those matters to their wives—especially where younger children and *girl things* were involved. If you're planning to have the children with you a lot, you're going to have to learn about these things. Ask yourself who your resources will be. Can you work with your children's mother to learn how to handle these things? Do you need to read some books about childhood development? Is there a family member who can be your counsel and guide?

If you are looking at the very real possibility of having joint custody of your kids, or even if you're just looking at having them with you on weekends, it would be wise to start lining up resource and support people whom you can call when you have questions. Parent groups are, of course, great resources.

IT'S NOT MY FAULT, DAD!

While addressed before, you need to get real about your child's emotions. This starts from before the divorce is even on the table. Age-appropriate explanations concerning the divorce will change over time. You may think that you've covered things well enough with your children, but it could be that you need to have the same conversation down the line when they've matured further mentally and emotionally. And sometimes, you may need to find other sources that can help match their comprehension.

Fred, a man who'd separated from his wife three years before, told the story of his ten-year-old son who had a particularly difficult time with his parents' divorce. For the first six months, Ian had fallen into a deep funk. He didn't want to talk about his parents' divorce. He sullenly told his father it didn't matter. Nothing mattered. "No, I'm not mad," he insisted, "and I'm not sad. It's no big deal. Just leave me alone."

Then one week during one of his visits, the boy came out of his room into the kitchen where Fred was fixing dinner. The boy reached up and put his hand on his father's shoulder.

"I just figured it out," Ian said.

"Figured what out?" Fred asked.

"It's not my fault, is it?"

"What's not your fault?" When he first heard these words, Fred wondered if Ian in trouble. That wasn't the case.

"You and Mom getting divorced," Ian said. "It wasn't my fault."

Fred turned off the stove and gave Ian a hug. Then, he steered Ian over to sit down at the kitchen table. "I didn't realize you ever thought you were to blame," Fred said. "I never blamed you, not in a million years. And I'm sure Mom didn't either. I'm so sorry if I ever gave you the impression that you might have even remotely been to blame."

"I know," Ian said. "I saw a program about it on TV."

Ian then told his father what had happened only minutes before. He had tuned in on a cable program where there was a roundtable discussion about children of divorce. Ian normally would have switched channels after coming across a program like this. This time, however, he'd come in on the middle of a discussion about children blaming themselves for their parents' breakups. Ian had listened with rapt attention. He'd never been able to articulate what he'd felt before this. Now, he not only had a way of talking about it, he had realized a truth, that kids do blame themselves for their parents' divorce though they are never at fault. It was as if a great weight had been lifted from his shoulders.

Once Ian's revelation completely sank in, there were a great many positive changes in his attitude toward both his parents. He rarely dropped into his silent withdrawals anymore. His sullenness was replaced by a much more outgoing attitude. And he began to settle down and make himself more at home at his father's small apartment.

The conflicts kids experience in divorce can be quite complicated, and few are ever resolved as easily as Ian's was, with the chance viewing of a special TV program. For that reason, if no other, it's important to know a little about the kinds of conflicts and anxieties kids are faced with. Here are seven big ones:

- Adjusting to the fact that Dad doesn't live with them anymore.

- Being angry with Dad for abandoning them—even though this might not be the case.

- Being angry with Dad because, "He must be the bad guy since he had to go away."

- Blaming themselves for the breakup.

- Adjusting to having two homes—one with Mom, one with Dad.

- Fearing that since Dad abandoned them, how can they be sure Mom won't go, too?

- Finding it difficult to be around Dad because he's always talking about how heartbroken he is over Mom divorcing him. (This makes kids feel they have to take sides.)

This constitutes only a very short list of the many ways that kids might be affected by divorce. I've listed these because they are mostly ones that, as adults, we might not even consider. For example, because you're so close to the real issues you had with your ex, it might never occur to you that your son or daughter might see himself or herself as the cause of your breakup. Similarly, it might never enter your mind that your kids would feel you had deliberately abandoned them. After all, you still talk to them on the phone several times a week, attend all their games, and see them at least on weekends. Where's the abandonment? However, even with all of that, they still can feel like you've walked out on their lives.

The home you make for yourself and for them can go a long way toward resolving many issues for children of divorce. When a child feels that he has a secure place with you in your home and that you are reasonably happy in this new place, modest though it might be, some of their concerns are ameliorated. But, be as attentive as you can to other issues that may be troubling them. We'll address signs of stress in this chapter, and steps you can take to minimize it. There's much that you can do to help your kids through these difficult times. Under ideal circumstances, you'd work with their mother on these issues. Consider the possibility of family counseling where your kids can meet with a counselor and either one or both of their parents.

BECOMING THE PARENT YOU WOULD LIKE TO BE

Within a few months after you complete the legal aspects of your divorce, you will begin to get somewhat settled into your life as a divorced father. While the initial crisis is beginning to fade, you may still be struggling with feelings stirred up by the breakup of your marriage and new ways of relating to your ex. Ready or not, it's time to embrace the work of building a positive and forward-looking extended family. You can now turn your attention to reflecting on the kind of parent you want to be, and what you want your new life to be.

There's a strong tendency following a divorce to give a great sigh of relief and then relax into accepting whatever comes. I believe we call that "going with the flow." But as a friend of mine recently pointed out, you'd better at least know which flow you're following. Some of them end up in pure crystalline lakes, some in oceans, and some in . . . well, I think you get the point. Go with the flow, but know the flow you're going with. If your kids are out there in the world, they'll be encountering infinite choices, opportunities, and influences. While you're a key influence in their lives, never forget that your children face a great many pressures and temptations that perhaps you will never know about.

Most parents don't develop a conscious plan on how they're going to raise their kids. However, when you've gone through a divorce and you've established two different households that the kids will identify as *home*, it isn't just enough to fly by the seat of your pants, as they say. A lot of what you do will, of course, will be responding to the needs of the moment. That's just part of life. But with two households involved, there are collaborative decisions to be made that will require planning ahead and defining expectations. You've got to set dates for when the kids will be with you and when they'll be with your ex. There may be issues around schooling or religious education that you'll need to work out. Schedules and decisions that may have happened more spontaneously when you were all together in one household might now have to be worked out months ahead, and that means *planning*. You have to be an intentional dad.

It may be that as parents become aware of the need to coordinate their schedules, they become increasingly aware that planning isn't limited to logistics.

Certainly, as parents we want to plan our lives so that we can be together and do things with our kids. And in terms of providing guidance, we want to help them make good choices and avoid making too many mistakes in their lives—especially those mistakes we made ourselves when we were kids! We may also put a high priority on openly communicating and treating each other with care, respect, and love. But these are mostly qualities and values that you can't force-feed. If you do, you'll usually get the opposite of what you had hoped for. These are qualities and values that arise from first building a solid foundation for your relationship.

TEACHING INTEGRITY

Integrity, the state of actually being what you present yourself to be and walking your talk, is not easy, especially during times of stress. It is important for fathers to do well on the integrity front whenever you possibly can. Some people subscribe to the *don't do as I do, do as I say* school of parenting. This is confusing to children, who can see that you do things and act in ways that you have tried to teach them are unacceptable.

Learning integrity is an important practice. Over time, disciplining yourself to live by your values and beliefs every moment of the day is one of life's greatest challenges. But the rewards are great, allowing you to feel more centered and whole and fully focused in your purpose. It's this wholeness that will deeply impress your own children. Out of their relationship with you, they will innately know how to create lives of their own that are focused in intent and happy.

If there is a singular goal where disciplining our kids is concerned, it is to teach them to choose well, to be true to themselves, and to hold a life course where their actions and thoughts help them to achieve their fondest dreams and aspirations. Discipline isn't just about having well-behaved kids; its ultimate goal and purpose is to raise kids who have an appreciation for creative and constructive thought and action, with an ability to honor others in the same ways that they honor themselves.

BUILDING TRUST AND ACCOUNTABILITY

Many times, children of divorce feel let down by their parents. It is so important for parents and children to have a relationship where communication is open and where your actions are predictable, reliable, and accountable. No matter what your justification for the divorce, it may well seem to your children that you let them down. When you're no longer there the hour they come home from school or when they go to bed at night or when they wake up on Christmas Day, they are probably going to feel you've abandoned them. If they don't have another explanation, they can make up the story themselves, creating villains in the family where there are none.

If you're the one with primary custody, the stories they put together are probably going to be very different. Don't be surprised if they wonder why Mom's not with them anymore. This reminds me of a story about a six-year-old child who believed that his father had sent his mother away to be adopted. This came about because he had a friend who had been adopted and he got the child's story a little mixed up. He didn't get straightened out on this until his seventh birthday when he said to his father, "I've got an idea. Let's adopt my mom!"

As your children put their own stories together around what has happened to their lives, it may or may not coincide with the actual facts as you know them. But the more accountable and open you can be in your daily communications and actions with your kids, the more they will come to see you as a source of security and dependable information in their lives.

Do you need to tell your children all the gory details of your divorce? No, and you probably shouldn't even attempt it until they are old enough to deal with adult issues. Chances are, those details won't even interest them by then. In the meantime, just assure them that even though Mom and Dad are no longer married, and that they live in different houses, you love them dearly, and so does Mom, and this will never change.

"My dad was a psychotherapist," a man in his mid-twenties recently shared with me. "He remarried a couple years after my parents' divorce. I wanted to live with him because Mom was a very difficult person. Dad and I talked on the phone two or three times a week all through my high school years, and mostly about Mom. Without ever once putting her down, as far as I can recall, he would assure me that Mom loved me. He'd tell me about different things I could try to make things go more smoothly between us. His suggestions didn't always work, but that was okay, somehow. I felt I had his support and that he cared enough for both Mom and me to never put her down."

By his language, staying uplifting, positive, loving, and offering advice to smooth over the challenging situations, this father created the perfect situation for his son to learn to trust and rely on his dad, even if he didn't live with him all the time.

You'll also find it's important for that trusting relationship to show up when you say you will, letting the kids know that their concerns come first for you, and that their time with you is quality time—not just party time. Any time you slip up with these foundational elements, without owning up to the mistake, you'll teach your children that they can't trust you to be there in times of crisis.

And crisis come! In his book *Live-Away Dads: Staying a Part of Your Children's Lives When They Aren't a Part of Your Home,* author William C. Klatte points out that children with little or no contact with their fathers are more likely to drop out of school and become involved in drug and alcohol abuse; girls are more likely to become pregnant as teens, and boys are more likely to become involved in crime and violence. If for no other reason, this should alert you, and every father, to the importance of being present in your kids' lives and doing everything in your power to be the best parent possible. Here are eleven ways you can do this:

1. Show an interest in what your children are doing at school and out of school. This includes helping with homework, watching or playing sports together, taking them to see movies, going to plays, planning a camping trip, or eating out.

2. Be available when your kids want to talk about the good, the bad, the sad, or the bewildering. If at all possible, don't say "in just a minute," or "not right now."

3. Regularly ask your children about their lives and the lives of their friends. Learn their friends' names. Know what fashions, music, television, and movies interest them. As they get older and begin thinking about such things, ask them about their hopes and dreams for the future, and what they'd like to see changed in the world.

4. Foster their courage, integrity, leadership, curiosity, and concern by sharing stories of how you or others have overcome great challenges or pursued areas of knowledge that were difficult. Teach them the joys of succeeding, but also support them when they fail, letting them know that both are part of life and are natural.

5. Be consistent, involved, aware, stable, and nurturing.

6. Avoid put-downs, judgmental tones, and unfair generalizations that show you're simply not listening.

7. Show a real interest in your teen's situation. Spend time listening; talk about anything and everything.

8. Respond to your teen's frustrating behavior by taking positive action and keeping an even temper. Both of these

may be difficult, but understand that your steadiness during this time of your children's lives is critical.

9. Calmly remind your teens of the established consistent rules, consequences, and responsibilities for their actions. If you haven't established clearly articulated rules and expectations for your teens' behavior, do so now.

10. Part of being a teenager is having a peer-centered language. You may, at times, feel your teens are talking in code. And you'll probably be right! Whatever it requires, committing the time and/or cracking the code will be a relationship builder.

11. Ask your teen what you can do to be more accessible to them when he or she needs to talk. If they don't know how to answer this—and they might not—ask other parents what they do, and seek outside resources such as parent seminars and books.

SOMETIMES THEY JUST DON'T LIKE YOU

On the path to building, or rebuilding, a relationship of trust with your kids, it's likely that you'll hit patches where they express dislike or hate for you. In the heat of a conflict, most of us tend to want to cast things in black and white. That's particularly true of younger kids. Under pressure, the first reaction is to look for a good guy and a bad guy to explain what happened and why. As a parent, you should prepare yourself for the fact that there will be times when you are assigned the role of the bad guy. Maybe

Mom tells your teenager they can't go to a certain concert because you said so. Or your child is told that the reason they can't afford "extras" is that you are stingy and don't give them enough money. (You may later discover, of course, that Mom actually said, "Your dad and I are having some financial difficulties right now, so you'll have to wait to save up your own money to buy that new computer game.") When you find you're the bad guy, be as direct as possible with the kids about your position. For example, you might tell your son, "I know you listen to this band, but I have heard them, and I don't like what they are putting out. Their attitudes toward women are mean and disgusting. Those aren't attitudes I can support or which I want my son to support." Once you've had your say, let your sons or daughters express themselves on this same issue. You will know how to take it from there.

If they decide, at this point, that you are still the villain, ask them how you can help them: "I know it's hard to tell your friends your dad won't let you go to the concert with them. Is there a way I might help you to deal with that?" Don't expect them to come up with a mature or appropriate request.

When and if you get to loggerheads, you only have a few choices:

- Try to find trust, compromise, and friendship in other aspects of your relationship; offer to compromise by helping them get tickets to a different concert that you can get behind, or coach them on how to manage with the allowance they have to get what they want.

- Actively try to change the child's mind or behavior: Ask them about how particular, inappropriate media (like music) makes them feel, and what it means to them. Ask about their expectations for finances, what their goals are, and how they think they can best achieve those dreams. Express why you have concerns, how you think those choices would effect your children, and how you would advise your child to experience the greatest success.

In the long run, your child will start to respond to you as you really are, rather than as some two-dimensional, cardboard model of you. As a result, the best thing you can do is give them your unequivocal opinions as well as your love, time, and energy.

On the flip side, there may be times when you don't much care for your children. When they hit the last of your triggers. Were you imagining things, or did your kid just act exactly like your ex? Don't be surprised.

You may be seeing things in your child that remind you of things you didn't like in your ex—or maybe even that you don't particularly like in yourself! Kids are great at mirroring their parent's best and worst traits and habits. Some of these traits skip around in the family, so maybe your child does something that reminds you of one of your own siblings or the child's grandparents. While these traits can be the source of wonder, they can also be the source of conflict for you, echoing back traits that you did not enjoy in your ex or in some other member of your family.

When Tyler got divorced, he became concerned when he noticed how much of his daughter's behavior was like her mom's. "Sonja is as stubborn and bull-headed as her mom. We get into it at least once every weekend she stays with me, and it's like being married to her mother all over again."

Tyler began locking horns with his daughter in much the same way he once had with his wife. He eventually did some work with a psychotherapist who helped him with this. "I was having one hell of a time with it," he explained. "Whenever Sonja and I got into a conflict, it opened up old wounds, and I found myself diving right into unfinished business with my ex. I had to take a close look at my own stuff and what I contributed to the problem. I eventually saw that Sonja is her own person and my issues aren't with her. When she gets into a stubborn streak, I can now address it as her and only her behavior, not all mixed up with the crap between her mother and me. And since I have been facing some of my own demons, it's going a lot better between my ex and me."

As he progressed in his understanding of how to deal with his daughter's stubborn behavior, he noticed that Sonja and her mother were also having problems. They had each found their match in the other. Equally stubborn, they also complained about the other's stubbornness, the very same trait that they themselves were most guilty of.

IT'S 10 P.M.: DO YOU KNOW WHERE YOUR KIDS ARE?

The kids are at their mother's. She's in charge now. You're thinking, "What good does it do me to even worry about them right now? I can't do anything about it." Right? Well, this might be technically true, but in the long run, you're going to eventually hear about it if they're getting into trouble—regardless of who is supposed to be looking after them. If you're smart, you'll keep in touch wherever they may be. That doesn't mean hovering over them or calling your ex every day or two for a report on the kids. Usually, this can be done through a phone call or text message now and then to just chat with your kids, let them know that you are there for them, and that you love them. You'd be surprised how much you can learn just by staying in touch in this way.

Many fathers pay for a cell phone for their children so that these regular contacts can be made easier between the child and Dad, without having to go through Mom. If you and their mom have an open, collaborative relationship, you may choose this. In this way, you can support each other in supporting the kids.

Your goal for keeping tabs on your kids is not aimed at totally controlling what they do. Rather, it's about staying close enough with them to catch developing problems early, presumably when they are easy to solve. Remember, you're dealing with teenagers here. In today's world, there's a *culture of adolescence* that poses a very powerful emotional influence on every teenager. While you can't protect your kids 100 percent from these influences, you may be able to either prevent or ameliorate serious problems such as pregnancies, addictions, and accidents.

As Teen Daughters Mature: As your daughter grows up, your relationship with her will change. She may no longer like the hugs and cuddles she enjoyed as a young child. Respect this as well as her need for privacy. Act in a caring manner. Showing an interest in what interests her will show her you still love her.

Most fathers are anxious and protective when their daughters begin dating. Allow her to make up her own mind about her relationships and listen to her when she needs someone to talk with. Your daughter will learn about positive male-female relationships by seeing you acting in a caring and respectful way to her mother and her. She needs your support rather than your disapproval.

And lots of dads are happy to leave the "girly" conversations to the mother, fearing the discomfort of the talks. No, it's not pleasant, but it certainly is important to dig in and do what is best for your daughter. Answer her questions (if you don't know, find out!), share your concerns, and listen to hers.

As Teen Sons Mature: It is all too easy, in the busy day-to-day routine of life, to overlook how important fathers are as role models for their teenage sons. Your son will watch you closely to learn about being a man, how to handle relationships and friendships, and what his role in society might be. If you expect your son to be socially responsible, he needs to see you embracing ethical and caring values as well as how to handle aggressive roles.

No doubt about it, being the parent of a teenage son can be very challenging, and may remind us of our own issues relating to the way we acted when we were that age. When your son messes up, teach him how to take responsibility; teach him how to make things right. When he is struggling, be a listening ear, empowering him to sort through his thoughts, choices, and consequences. When he needs to relieve the stress of being a teenager, teach him healthy means of blowing off steam—maybe paired with teaching valuable skills.

The teen years can be a time for fathers and sons to build long-lasting bonds, mutual trust, love, and support.

WATCH FOR STRESS IN THE TEEN YEARS

Short of living in an active combat zone, divorce is on every psychologist's list one of the biggest stressor most of us will ever experience in life. For kids, especially younger ones, it represents a critical rip, hole, or tear in the fabric of their worlds. As one woman put it, reflecting on the divorce of her parents when she was twelve, "It pulled the cosmic carpet right from under my feet, and I found myself flailing around in space all through my adolescence."

Clearly, divorce can add much stress to a young person's life. Stressing over the possibility of your child experiencing stress will only exaggerate the problem. If nothing else, remember that divorce is an experience that large numbers of children are living with, and most end up doing just fine. Your job now is to provide a stable and loving home, using your good judgment about when to line up special help. This judgment is based on *knowing the signs* of when your kids are stressed out and struggling.

Kids express their emotional difficulties differently than most adults do. Usually when an adult starts to get depressed, symptoms can include alterations of usual sleep patterns, increase or decrease of appetite, mood swings, decreased energy, lowered sex drive, and lack of interest in the world around them. A child getting depressed may or may not show these symptoms, but there will be more of a tendency for a depressed child to get increasingly belligerent or even combative, acting out in a number of aggressive ways.

Kids are individuals, and when they are stressed out, they will respond in ways that are unique to them. Signs aren't always clear in children, but certainly should cause you to investigate further. If your child's school grades drop, be on the alert for other signs of stress. At the opposite pole, if your child is a high achiever and she starts spending significantly more time studying, that could be either a sign of stress or of a healthy increase in their interest in a particular subject. Similarly, if he is into extracurricular activities, such as soccer or other sports, and he starts turning more and more of his attention to them, recognize that this could be a symptom of either stress or increased drive.

Many kids may just want to be with their friends in times of stress, while others isolate themselves in their rooms and play video games or read books all day long. There are the ones who burn off their stress with lots of activity and exercise, and others who turn into couch potatoes, their eyes glued to the TV. Under stress, children tend to develop tunnel vision, narrowing their range of interest and activity. This can often pass as the child becomes more disciplined in whatever they are doing, but the danger is that, given enough stress, kids will narrow their horizons rather than expand them, thus limiting their development.

You need to pay attention to the possibility of abnormal responses to the stress your children are experiencing. This is especially true if personality disorders, abuse, or other psychiatric problems have been part of the family history. Even if these past problems are now absent, it is possible for a child to get into serious emotional trouble when stressed. If you see signs of the more serious problems, get your child evaluated by a mental health professional.

What are the red flags that mark the difference between *normal* stress responses and more serious issues? The following list can help you determine that, but use your best judgment as you attempt to apply them:

Grades at School: It's common for grades to drop some during the throes of a divorce, but if it looks like they fell off a cliff, and the child is in danger of not passing, definitely step in and talk with your child's teacher and guidance counselor. Find out what's going on at school, how your child is acting in class, and get their suggestions for what you might do.

Acting Out and Conduct Problems: There are a number of things that can lead to conduct problems. These include ineffective discipline, hanging out with a bad peer group, the child struggling with a serious emotional trauma, drug use, or an onset of mood disorders such as depression or bipolar disorder. Suffice it to say, if these symptoms are getting out of hand, or if the child is going to get entangled in the legal system, seek professional help.

If you sense trouble, learn as much as you can about the situation, and spend a lot more time with your child, talking with him or her whenever you are together. It's common for a teen that is getting into trouble to be sullen and uncommunicative. Just arrange more family outings; tell your child you love him or her, but don't expect or demand a lot of feedback, or you may be disappointed.

Hanging with a Bad Crowd: Who does your child associate with? Do you know his or her friends? If you do not pay attention to such things, you are likely to get blindsided someday soon by trouble you didn't see coming. Parents' intuition about their kids' friends is one of the most important tools you have. Should your child be mixed up in a truly bad crowd, you will probably find yourself in the unenviable position of trying to control your child's social life.

Once the trouble starts, you may want to begin by telling your kid that you are concerned about the people he's spending time with and you want him to stay away from that crowd. More often than not, you're going to have a rebellion on your hands, but be as clear and honest as you can be with him or her. Let him know that you are concerned about him, and not that you are arbitrarily trying to restrict his activities or friendships. If this doesn't work, it leaves you in a power struggle with a rapidly physically maturing adolescent, who probably isn't on the same page as you about developing collaborative relationships. Even if he says he will modify his behavior, be very wary until you actually see the promised change.

At this point, you come to a difficult decision. You can resort to more militant disciplinary actions. Or, especially he or she is getting close to adulthood, you may be forced to let go, simply watching your child continue to make decisions that limit his or her future potential. Many older children will go through rather dark times when you feel they are completely lost to you. But just as many come back around, for no particular reason that you can discern. Children, after all, have their own lives, and most are far more resourceful than most parents can imagine.

Drugs and Alcohol: In this day and age, it's a rare teenager who doesn't experiment with some type of mind-altering substance. Most teens' experimentation only goes so far, and they decide that whatever kick they get out of drugs or alcohol isn't worth the trouble it causes them. Others, unfortunately, get more deeply involved and endanger themselves by associating with criminal elements. Drug use can be behind symptoms as far ranging as moodiness and acting out. Addiction is a serious illness, endangering physical and psychological health, the ability to work or go to school, and destroying relationships and capacity for intimacy. If drugs or alcohol seem to be an issue, you and your child should see a mental health professional. Involvement in a 12-step program, or similar peer-run recovery group, may also be helpful.

DISCIPLINE: WHAT WORKS AND WHAT DOESN'T

Can we agree that children need guidance and discipline? Probably. Yet the techniques and styles of discipline are as individual as the people who practice them. Do what works for you, but always remember that in anything you do, you are modeling behavior that your child will copy and mirror back in his relationships with you and others. A child who experiences harsh and painful punishment will often inflict similar punishment on those around him; this could be a sibling, his friends, a person he simply doesn't like, or even you and his mom.

The message you want to get across to your kid is simple enough; you want to point them in the direction of acting in ways that will get them what they truly want and which will benefit them in the years to come. What you don't want is to create an ongoing power struggle. You want your interventions to achieve the following:

- They should have a positive emotional impact on the child.

- They should send a clear message that you are in control of the situation.

- The positive results of the disciplinary action should far outweigh the negative.

- You can both forgive and move on.

Whatever disciplines you impose, children need to be able to predict what to expect for their behavior. Be as consistent as possible. Define your expectations by writing down your rules in simple language and periodically going over them with your children. Post the rules and expectations on the refrigerator door or some other place that both you and your kids can have access to.

When there's a violation of the written rules, ask the child if he remembers that rule. If there is any doubt, read it back to him from the list. You can point out that he might forget the rule for the first couple of times, but after that, it's up to him to be responsible and honor that rule. If he doesn't take responsibility for himself, then you will have to take that responsibility for him—and he might not like the way you take responsibility. In this way, you're teaching him not only to obey the rules, but to make choices about self-responsibility.

After all, one of the key understandings of any social order is that the society demands a certain level of responsibility on the part of every citizen, and when those responsibilities aren't met, society will jump in and either punish the violation or demand retribution. As one father put it, "We need to learn that we have a choice—either we take responsibility for our own actions or someone else will! And when it's the latter, we have lost control of our lives."

Many parents I've spoken with like to offer their children some choice over how and when the consequences of their actions are to be meted out. Be very careful of this. An example is when a child's punishment involves doing extra chores around the house. Experienced parents will tell you that most children will procrastinate as long as possible, sometimes with the hope that if they delay long enough, they'll wear you down and they'll get out of having to do what they've been asked to do. So, choose wisely and avoid choices that get you into power struggles with children. As a child psychologist friend recently advised, "Pick your battles so that you won't lose."

What's a battle that you can't lose? If your child has his own phone, take it away for a week. Does she have car privileges? Take away her key. Are there special programs he likes to watch on TV? Well, too bad. The TV is off limits as a consequence of some unacceptable behavior.

The more immediate the consequences, the better for everyone. Provide your child with minimal opportunities to change the rules on you. If you ground a child for two weeks, that means you become his jailer, and you had better be willing to stand guard twenty-four hours a day, seven days a week. Is this how you wish to spend your time? Probably not. But if you are a person who works at home, it may be a reasonable restriction. Just be forewarned to give that lump a poke that appears to be your daughter sleeping soundly in her bed. Chances are, she's pulled the oldest trick in the game, stuffing pillows under the blankets to make it appear that she's asleep, then hopping out the window. Where is she? Well, probably at the concert you forbade her to attend.

Avoid setting up consequences that will take place too far in the future. Kids experience time very differently than adults do, especially younger kids. Next weekend can seem like next year or forever and ever in your child's mind. It's just much better to keep the punishment brief and swift, served out within the same time period that the offense occurred, or at least within a couple of hours or days. In that way, you and your child can move on to the fun things in your relationship. Nobody wants to mope around all grumpy for hours or days waiting for the consequences.

So, you've decreed a penalty for your child's unacceptable be-havior. From this point, erase the situation from your mind. You want your child to have an image of him or herself as a really great kid who, sometimes, like the rest of us, strays from the path. The moment he or she is back on track put all the discipline stuff behind you. Drop it. You have a great kid; focus on that. Let them know that you love them, believe in them, and think they are the greatest.

With all this talk about the various problems of fatherhood and building a healthy extended family, it's all too easy to overlook the joys and experiences of deep intimacy and love that are part of raising kids. I've challenged you to get real about the situation your kids are in or that they will face. And most of what we've explored in this chapter is about the difficulties, with some rough guidelines about how to keep things running smoothly. Be careful, as you read these guidelines, to remember that your highest goal will be to enjoy being a father and having your children love, respect, and enjoy being with you. Learning to handle the challenges is an integral part of creating the space in your lives where you can be vulnerable and open to the pleasures of each other's company.

CHAPTER EIGHT:

KEEPING YOURSELF TOGETHER

"Each of you is perfect the way you are . . .
and you can use a little improvement."
—Shunryu Suzuki, Roshi

Unless you're superhuman, you are likely to be feeling overwhelmed at this point in your divorce. You're getting used to living alone in a new place. You might be working two jobs—or, at least, one and a half. Money problems are accumulating, your kids are acting up, your ex is on your case nearly every day, and your girlfriend just dumped you because she thought you were too melancholy.

There's a huge amount of stress in those first months of a separation. Recognizing and managing it is the name of the game.

What's more, there are endless challenges to be met if you are going to handle things collaboratively with your ex-spouse, and you'd better be at your best for that. You're going to be carrying around a lot of stress no matter what you do, but if you're not doing something to minimize the load, any efforts to collaborate are going to turn into battles—either with yourself or with your loved ones, and maybe both.

STRESS RAISES ITS UGLY HEAD AND SMIRKS

Before you can manage your stress, you have to be able to recognize it, and in the modern world, where stress is just a way of life, we've become so good at pretending it isn't there that most of us don't even know what to look for, or how to evaluate the level we're dealing with. To assist you, here's a short list of symptoms to look out for:

- Muscular tension, particularly in arms, legs, back, and chest.

- Back ache or tight shoulder and neck muscles.

- Loss of appetite or overeating.

- Sleeplessness.

- Constant worry or going over and over arguments and inequities in your mind.

- Jumpiness or reactiveness.

- Short on patience.

- Short tempered. (See a psychotherapist if you find yourself out of control, such as doing something to harm yourself or others.)

- Inability to concentrate.

- Missing or forgetting deadlines (such as paying bills, missing appointments, etc.)

- Distractedness (drifting off at meetings or during conversations with friends.)

- Disorientation (forgetting directions to a familiar place.)

- Difficulty working or playing with others.

- Abuse of drugs or intoxicants (including prescription drugs) to help you cope.

- Elevation of blood pressure (get a blood pressure cuff and monitor it regularly if you are concerned—and see your doctor if this has been an issue in the past.)

- Depression or lethargy (see a psychotherapist if it persists or gets worse.)

- Loss of motivation. (Often a form of depression.)

- Frightening dreams that wake you up.

- Withdrawal from social interactions.

- Susceptibility to colds or other infections.

- Aggravation of allergies.

- Difficulty digesting food, diarrhea, stomach distress or cramps, constipation.

- Sexual dysfunction or loss of interest in sex (impotence, inability to climax, etc.).

If you find yourself suffering from four or more of these symptoms, it means your stress levels are over the top, and it is time to look at what you can do to manage it. As you seek ways to do this, educate yourself about what stress is and how it works, both mentally and physically. Understand that it is not just a mental thing; rather, it involves your entire body and mind. It begins as a psychophysical response to a perceived threat which triggers the fight or flight response. That fight or flight response is hardwired into you and is the key mechanism by which your body and mind alerts you to dangers and keeps you from getting hurt. The most basic responses to a perceived threat, controlled by this inherent mechanism of self-protection, are to either defend or fight, or to run.

In either case, there are a number of physiological changes triggered by the perception of a threat: adrenal hormones are sent into the bloodstream, causing blood flow to increase to the big muscles such as legs, arms, and back. These same hormones change your brain and body chemistry, causing you to become hyper alert and hyper responsive. All of these changes are designed to prepare you to either run or fight.

According to Arthur Guyton, M.D. (*Textbook of Medical Physiology*), the following organs and organ systems undergo dramatic changes whenever the fight or flight response is activated:

blood vessels, sweat glands, large muscles, eyes, brain, heart, lungs, stomach, portions of the intestines, kidneys, bladder and urinary tract, genitals, and anal sphincter. If stress is prolonged, as it is in the case of a divorce, the immune system will also be affected. Since the immune system protects us from infection and is implicated in allergic responses, it helps to account for symptoms such as increased colds or difficulties with allergies. Notice the close relationship between this list of organ and organ systems and the list of symptoms above.

We are more likely to override the fight or flight response as we attempt to seek more reasonable or peaceful solutions. While this certainly has its advantages, it also results in our holding much of our stress in our bodies and minds. We stuff our emotions or the problems mount up until the mere realization of all we have to handle itself becomes the tiger lurking in the jungle and threatening to devour us. The bottom line is that we end up living our lives as if we are under attack 24/7—and that's *chronic, prolonged anxiety*. And we cannot expect to be healthy, responsive, and reasonable to deal with under those circumstances.

If the threat is such that you don't know how to handle it, or normal fight and flight responses are not appropriate— as is the case with most matters of the heart—then another response may come into play: depression. Depression is often characterized by a particular way of thinking—i.e., that the problem you're confronting is hopeless, that nothing can be done to make a bad situation better, or that you are incapable of changing anything, and the world holds no promise of anything pleasant for you. What results is a dulling of virtually all experience and a kind of circular thinking that keeps us trapped in our own hopelessness.

Ten Not-So Hard-and-Fast Rules for Handling Stress

1. Focus on things as they are right now instead of dwelling on the past or worrying about the future. Keep in mind that you cannot control either the past or the future. You can help to shape your future, but you can do so only one small step at a time.

2. Take one thing at a time. You may be facing what seems like an infinite number of challenges at the moment, and they can all seem to roll into one huge mass that threatens to run right over you. Instead of lumping everything together in one big ball, take one thing at a time.

3. Ask for advice instead of complaining. In talking with close friends and relatives, try not to burden them with your complaints and troubles. Instead, ask for their advice and listen to their ideas and any wisdom they might offer.

4. Act on your decisions. Whenever you have come to a decision about a challenge you can actually do something about, act on it now and do so resolutely. Taking positive action builds trust in your ability to have an impact on your future.

5. Keep yourself constructively occupied. Be with other people at this time, preferably in situations such as volunteer work or athletic events where short-term accomplishments are promised. Find activities where you can feel useful.

6. Practice forgiveness. Holding onto judgment and blame, even though you have been hurt in some way, accomplishes nothing and only erodes your own mental health. Look for books or seek spiritual guidance if you find yourself in a blaming posture.

7. Conscious relaxation. Seek ways to consciously relax for a period of at least twenty minutes each day. This can be anything from going for a walk where you can concentrate on the natural beauty around you to listening to music or meditation practice.

8. Establish a daily routine and stick to it. Create structure in your life, perhaps around meals or other routine events, since it helps to foster a sense of security at a time when life itself seems to have become uprooted.

9. Unwind a few hours before you go to bed. Put a curfew on any thoughts about your troubles or their solutions. Put them out of mind after 8 p.m. And if you wake up in the middle of the night, listen to a relaxation CD or soothing music instead of dwelling on problems.

10. Yield to crisis. It's not always easy to recognize when we're in crisis. The telltale signs are feeling overwhelmed or unable to know where to even begin to solve our problems. Don't cling to attitudes of "toughing it out." Rather, admit to being overwhelmed and seek help from a counselor, therapist, or physician to give you a hand over this rough spot.

Doctors warn that when our stress levels are particularly high—as they most certainly are in divorce—we're susceptible to certain illnesses. These may include gastrointestinal complaints, sexual problems, irritable bladder, skin problems, anxiety or depression, mouth ulcers, aggravation of symptoms if you are asthmatic, attacks of angina or disturbances of heart rate, muscular problems such as "nervous tics," and even certain forms of baldness (alopecia areata).

While you may not be able to immediately stop all the events in your life that are causing you stress, you can learn to manage stress levels during this period of your life so that their impact on your health and your ability to function well are not threatened. This is a particularly good time to look at your diet; your exercise

levels; your use of alcohol or other drugs; and your intake of caf-
feine, which can have a powerful impact on your nervous system,
leading to shakiness, sleep deprivation, and irritability.

You want to be healthy, but your kids need you to be. They
want to feel secure in knowing you'll be there for them, able to
participate in the joys of family.

IN THE EVENT THAT
WE LOSE CABIN PRESSURE

Remember the little speech always delivered by the flight attendant when your plane takes off from the airport?

*Should the cabin lose pressure, oxygen masks will drop down. If you are
traveling with a child or an adult who might need assistance, secure your own
mask before helping others' with theirs.*

On the surface, this sounds pretty self-serving, to take care of
yourself before helping others. But it is based on the concept that
if you are going to be truly helpful, you'd better first make sure you
are coming from a place of strength. In a depressurized cabin at
20,000 feet elevation, one can become totally disoriented, go into
a panic, or completely lose consciousness quickly.

It can be useful to look at the same principle in times of family
crisis. If you are floundering, you will be in no position to help
your children. To be their strength and morale-booster during
this time, you will have to be pretty solid within yourself. For this
reason, taking the time to take care of yourself isn't a luxury or
a personal indulgence; it's a necessity, particularly when you are
responsible for other people who are, because of their youth or
infirmity, dependent on you.

So be selfish in order that you might be better able to offer the strength, support, and willing guidance that the younger members of your family will require. How do you do this when there may be seemingly endless demands on your time and resources? It comes down to prioritizing, by making lists of the tasks and responsibilities you're faced with and making some choices. This is "triage" time, that is, time to sort out: a) what absolutely needs to be given top priority; b) what can wait until certain top priorities are served; and c) what you can let slip, if need be. In other words, choose your problems rather than thinking you have got to get them all done at once.

There are dozens of courses offered on the topic of stress management, but it all boils down to this: you can only handle so much at any given time. If you try to take on too much, something will give, and it could be your health or your family relationships. And if you push it too far, taking on too much can cost you your sanity.

What is too much? That may be the $64,000 question. In the midst of divorce, even the most basic task can seem like too much. The message is that divorce is already an overload and whatever choices you can make that lessen the burden, the better off you'll be.

Most men don't take the time to develop a big picture about what has to be done and then set up clear priorities for accomplishing them. We tend to take care of whatever is most pressing or glaring in the moment. It's the old *squeaky-wheel-gets-the-grease* principle of management. This can be okay when stress levels aren't too high or prolonged and you know there will be time, energy, and resources to knock off each task as it comes. However, divorce has a way of heaping on new tasks at an alarming rate.

So, if you follow the squeaky wheel system of management, there's a good chance you're going to quickly get behind. Once you're behind, it's easy to feel like things are hopeless, and everything you touch becomes not just a job to accomplish, but also an affliction. One thing's for certain: any ideals you had about being collaborative in the divorce flies out the window. You simply can't find the emotional fortitude to collaborate when you're feeling buried alive. You go into survival mode where nobody matters but yourself, not even your kids.

Before things have piled up too high, step back for a look at the big picture. Then, sit down and make up a list so that you can prioritize, dedicating the most energy to the things that will have the greatest positive impact in the long run. In case you're hovering around that place where you don't even know exactly where to begin, here's a sample list of all the things you might be juggling at this time:

- Work issues

- Budgeting and other money issues

- Quality time with the kids

- Legal issues and hassles

- Interpersonal problems

- Personal needs

- Social time

- Home maintenance

- Overcoming bad personal habits to establish constructive new behavior

Each of these categories can, and usually do, include, a complex of issues. For example, the issue of your work might include anything from the fact that you are looking for a job, or a better job, to your level of satisfaction with the work you're doing. Work issues might spill over into other categories on this list as well. For example, Gene's work as a sales representative often required him to be out of town for two-week periods. This meant that scheduling time with his kids was a problem. Flying back for the weekend to be with them was expensive and the extra travel was hard on Gene himself. He eventually worked out new schedules with his employer that minimized the number of weekends he'd be away, and he scheduled regular phone calls or video chats with the kids for those days he was on the road.

Use the list above as a way to get started on your own priority list. As you look over the items you've listed, ask yourself questions about each one that will reveal to you where you should put it on your priority list. If you have a friend to brainstorm with, rally their aid. Here are six key questions you might ask yourself:

1. How urgent is it to address this issue right now?

2. Who or what will be affected if I ignore this category f or now?

3. Is it important to invest a significant portion of my time and resources on this issue right now?

4. What would happen if I simply crossed this category off my list right now? Who would be affected? What consequences, if any, would there be?

5. What is the big picture on this issue? Is this one of those things that might come back to bite me in the butt somewhere down the line if I don't do anything about it right now? Will putting it off have a negative effect on relationships that are important to me? Am I missing anything?

6. Can this be solved by looking for alternatives outside the box? (For example, when Howard found he had to fully furnish his new apartment and had no money to do it, he invited his friends to a housewarming party and asked them to bring along any furnishings they wanted to get rid of. Overnight, he ended up with everything he needed to make his new home quite comfortable. Eclectic, yes, but comfortable.)

Ask each of these questions with an open mind. It may be difficult to hold your focus on some of them, either because they hold an emotional charge for you or because you simply don't feel like thinking about that group of issues right now. Nevertheless, the sooner you can deal with them, clearly thinking about each item, and setting priorities for getting them done, the better off you'll feel.

Having a vague to-do list hovering around in your brain can be a terrible energy drain and source of anxiety. What happens is that everything gets exaggerated. Shakespeare wrote, "There is nothing either good or bad, but thinking makes it so." If you've got a long list of things piling up in your mind, chances are that the weight of that pile is going to turn your thinking sour. If your list is set up so that you have a plan and a timetable for getting things done, you can focus your thinking on constructive ways to complete your tasks. You'll soon discover that this kind of constructive thinking greatly reduces worry and tension.

As you become more comfortable with the items you're dealing with, set your tasks up according to the following three Tracks of Action:

Track A: Things that need both your immediate and ongoing attention, without which there will be unacceptable consequences.

What to do: Give this track your full attention, starting right now—even if it is just jotting down how you will accomplish your first steps.

Track B: Things that need your attention eventually, but can wait for now.

What to do: Make notes about how long you can safely put off attending to the items for this track. Note that you are not ignoring these tasks. You will make a plan for when and how you will be attending to them, even if it is at some time in the future.

Track X: Write down things that you can safely ignore till Hell freezes over, either with no major consequences or with consequences that you and others can live with.

What to do: Cross out everything that you can honestly say belongs on this list.

Take this process of sorting out your to-do lists seriously and take your time with it. You'll be surprised at how beneficial it can be to spend just an hour working with your lists and becoming thoroughly acquainted not only with what you need to do but how you are going to do it and when.

You may want to break Track A into smaller bites as you go along. Maybe you'll even discover that there are items within items that you will need to place on this track or that you can shift over onto Track B or even Track X. If so, go ahead and make those shifts right away.

If you find things on Track A that have a heavy emotional charge for you, it may be because you are predicting less than a positive outcome on them. For example, Gene, in our anecdote above, was concerned that if he missed his weekend visits with his kids because of the times his work took him out of town, his ex-wife might use this against him, claiming he was being an irresponsible dad. While he'd already had several talks with her about this matter, nothing positive had come of them. He realized that having another discussion with her was not going to be the best use of his time, and that he'd probably fail in his efforts. After some inner debate with himself, he decided to delegate the matter to his attorney. While his attorney felt this was not altogether necessary, he did it anyway, which freed Gene of the stress he was feeling around negotiating the matter with his ex.

The lesson Gene's story offers is that delegating some matters to other people is sometimes the best way to go. It may be a professional person to whom you can delegate, a close friend who views himself as your advocate, or a trusted family member who is not afraid to discuss the matter with your ex. You may find, as others before you have, that family members or friends who are close to you are also close to your ex-spouse. If that's the case, this person just might be a good mediator between you and your spouse. Don't disregard it as a possibility.

Another tactic to keep in mind as you go through your lists is to play with worst-case scenarios. And I do mean *play*. Take it lightly. On the surface, this might seem like it could be anxiety producing. But the point of this exercise is to make decisions about what you can live with and what you can't.

Chances are quite good that even your *worst*-case scenarios may turn out much better than you might have imagined. In many cases, the solutions do involve lifestyle changes.

Changes can be tough, that's true. However, parents and children faced with unexpected changes may just find that the alternatives are more worthwhile than the original plan. Play with the options, rather than allowing the rerouting to escalate stress.

Modest Proposals and Tips

- When you're feeling stuck or overwhelmed, reach out for help. Ask someone whose judgment you trust for suggestions or advice.

- When faced with issues that are so emotionally charged that you can't get even close to making a solid decision, seek out the assistance of a professional counselor.

- Put your energy into efforts that can get better. Don't put time into lost causes, no matter how idealistic you may feel about them. If in the future you have the resources to return to that effort, go back to it, this time with personal reserves that can put you in a good position to succeed.

- Look carefully at your personal lifestyle demands. Is it possible that you are living beyond your present means? Are the ideals you maintain around your material existence exerting too great a cost? From where in your life are those ideals exacting their price? From your emotional health? From your spiritual well-being? From nurturing social or interpersonal relationships? Examine the tradeoffs carefully and make more informed choices.

If you hope to reduce the stress you are feeling around the journey you've embarked on the day you and your wife separated, choosing to shift your energy toward the completion of the items on your priority lists is going to be critical. Remind yourself that your feelings are your feelings, and that, regardless of the external events that may seem to have created them, you are the author of whatever dark feelings you are experiencing. Can you let them go? You can if you start shifting your perspective on those feelings, seeing that you are their author, regardless of how clear it might seem that what you are experiencing is caused by external events.

FOLLOWING THE PATH OF POSITIVE TRANSFORMATION

Think of this as a time to rebuild your life through more conscious choices and decisions. Look for activities in your community, or among your circle of friends, that will nurture you emotionally, spiritually, physically, and intellectually. Whatever you do along these lines will help to ease the stress you are experiencing. But broaden your perspectives even here, thinking of these new activities not only as addressing the problems of stress but also as opening you to new possibilities and opportunities for meeting new people, expanding your knowledge, and having some fun and adventure.

Look around for programs that can do all this while combating any depressive moods you might be experiencing. Consider tai chi, yoga, walking, jogging, running, hiking, biking, swimming, weight training, aerobics, dancing, meditation, and relaxation training. Spend time alone in the country or on a mountain. Sometimes, the best thing to do is right here at home, curling up with a good book, taking art courses, learning to play a musical instrument, taking a cruise, joining a book group, a soccer team, a local drama group, etc. Take up an activity that you've dreamed of doing, but have not had the time for. Maybe you've dreamed of writing poetry or a book, or building wood furniture.

Find out what's available in your community around such activities as those listed above. Look into your community colleges or even take a course online. The world is filled with opportunities such as these. If your motivation is presently low, or even non-existent, have patience, but also keep your eyes and ears open for that class or group that piques your interest or even your passion.

STEPS TOWARD COLLABORATION AND ALLOWING OTHERS TO HELP

Sometimes, as we are doing our best to keep the collaborative process alive and well, we just run out of gas. At such times, we need people around us to offer a helping hand. Keep in mind that just as you gain pleasure from helping others, so too can others gain pleasure from helping you. You've got to let them know what you need, however, and you do that by simply asking.

When you ask for help, even if it's just for ten minutes of emotional support over the phone, make sure you are choosing people who are open to helping you and who can offer the kind of support you need at that moment. At the same time, be certain that you keep the relationship reciprocal. Friends want to know that we care about them, even during those times when we are reaching out for their assistance.

In a truly collaborative divorce, the ex-partners do what they can to support one another, knowing that doing so ultimately benefits the kids. When one or the other of you is in need, look for ways to be helpful, even as you maintain clear boundaries that say, "While we have terminated our marriage relationship, I care how you are doing and want you to be healthy and happy." True, this can be a definite challenge in the beginning, but you have only to turn that thought around to understand its benefit. Imagine your ex saying that same thing to you, and really take it in. Somewhere on the other side of the tension, you are presently feeling and the moment you can at last see yourself and your ex in a new light—just two people doing their best to make their ways in the world—you can at least entertain the possibility of collaboration and start moving in that direction. Make the decision to hold the intention of giving and receiving help from your ex, knowing you are both in need of support at this time, and you'll be making an important forward stride.

This could be that your ex allows a little extra flexibility on the time the kids spend with you while you process things. Or, perhaps, she helps you talk to the kids about changing expectations, plans for making the best of downsizing, and increasing compassion and play as the whole family adjusts to the new situation.

Keeping it together is important for yourself and for your children. Things are turbulent, and this means you need to protect your own well-being so that you can be available to your kids. Above all, remember what the flight attendant advised about taking care of yourself first—*secure your own mask before helping others with theirs.*

CHAPTER NINE:

BIRTHDAYS AND HOLIDAYS

"The best portion of a good man's life is his little, nameless,
unremembered acts of kindness and of love."
—William Wordsworth

Birthday parties and holidays can be really tough the first year or so after your divorce, particularly if you spend them without your children. And even if you and your spouse have been through a difficult divorce and are still angry at each other, you can miss her as well. Why? Perhaps because each time you think of holidays and birthdays you spent together in better times, you are reminded of disappointments and dreams you once shared. But take heart, because as each year passes, you and your family will become more comfortable with the new family structure and likely will create new rituals and ways to celebrate important events together.

Holidays are, after all, the times we ordinarily set aside to relax, celebrate the lives of our loved ones, recharge our batteries, and let go of our everyday burdens. While this might be our intention, holidays are usually difficult for divorced families, and parents can easily become self-centered and bummed out, and either consciously or unconsciously create a stressful atmosphere.

You may lose your spouse when you divorce, but you'll never lose the responsibility of being a strong, compassionate, and collaborative parent. You and your ex-spouse will always be your children's parents, so do everything you can to honor your children's relationship with their mother, regardless of how you might be feeling about her for now. If the kids express a strong desire to spend their holidays and birthdays with her, understand the importance of allowing them to do just that. This is when your collaborative parenting skills come into play. While you cannot undo the divorce for the holidays, there are proactive things you can do and thoughtful, collaborative ways you can act.

HAVE A HAPPY BIRTHDAY

What are the expectations around birthdays—for you, for your ex, and for your children? And how do divorced parents handle the conflicts which inevitably arise around these personal holidays? Adjustments around your extended family aren't always easy, since several people, at least, are usually involved in the arrangements. Knowing what others have done isn't always helpful, but that knowledge can provide options for you to choose from.

In most cases, the parent with whom the child is staying when his or her birthday comes around is the one who gives the party. If that's you, make certain you invite your child's mother and welcome her warmly to the party. If there's still a good deal of strain between you and your ex, this may be a problem. In that case, consider the possibility of discussing the matter with your ex. If you or your ex don't feel comfortable with her attending the party you are giving, or vice versa, then look at the possibility of your having separate parties.

"The first couple years after our divorce," Terry explained, "my ex and I couldn't stand to be in the same room together, so inviting each other to parties we had for Tessa was out of the question. Things are better now, but negotiating what to do at first was sheer misery. We finally agreed to have separate parties and sometimes, a week or two would fall between Tessa's mom's party and mine. But that didn't matter to Tessa. In fact, I'm sure she liked the idea of having her birthday celebrated twice. Things have softened up a lot between her mom and me since then, but Tessa still likes what we've come to call *the two-party system*."

Sometimes, the age of your children will pretty much dictate some of the choices you make around birthdays.

Kids Five and Under: Younger children usually live with the custodial parent where they have all their stuff—clothes, toys, and friends. In the majority of cases in the U.S., the mother has custody of the toddler, though there are certainly a significant number of exceptions. If you're in a situation where your child is with her mom, negotiate in a respectful manner for an invitation to the birthday party. If you get invited, don't detract from the joy of the day, or you will likely never be invited again. Volunteer to bring treats and/or help with the birthday tasks and errands. If you or your ex only feel comfortable with your being at the party for a short period of time—maybe just long enough to deliver a present, a kiss to the birthday child, and give a cheerful celebratory face—that's what you should do.

Kids Six and Older: In most cases, older kids are going to gravitate toward where the fun is. If your children's best friends are living in Mom's neighborhood, chances are pretty good that this is where your kids will want to be on their birthdays. If your child really wants to be with Mom on their special day, even though they are scheduled to be at your house, let them go and don't guilt trip them about it. And don't take this as a personal betrayal or indication that they don't like you as much as they like their mom. They might just like Mom's cooking better. Or maybe right now they are simply more comfortable being with Mom. It happens, even when families are all together under a single roof and everyone is happy with each other. This is something most parents must come to terms with, regardless of whether there's been a divorce or not.

The bottom line is this: Don't mess up your child's birthday. It's their day, so do everything in your power to make it memorable and fun. This is no time for pouting or guilt tripping.

Maybe you're the party host this time. Remember to invite the other parent. If you're the guest, relax and enjoy the party.

HINTS FOR SUCCESSFUL BIRTHDAYS AND HOLIDAYS

Here are some guidelines to help get you through the birthdays and holidays with as little damage and as much joy and as possible.

Be Flexible: "Grandma's coming to my party!"

Those words, uttered by your young daughter over the phone, may be wonderful news for her, but not for you. Grandma, your ex's mother, can't stand the sight of you. For weeks, you've been planning a birthday party for your daughter at your house. It is, after all, her time to be with you. But now, with Grandma on the way, your own party is going to get sandbagged. Was this deliberate on Grandma or your ex's part? Maybe, but don't put your attention there. If your daughter is going to enjoy her special day, she'll want to be with Grandma. And that means the party will be at your ex's. Are you going to put up a fuss? Well, you won't if you have your daughter's best interests at heart. Your daughter is overjoyed at the prospect of Grandma being at her party, and you're not going to spoil that. This is just the reality you have to work with.

Plans need to change in response to the unexpected. Why does the need to be flexible always seem to fall in your camp? Where your children's birthdays are concerned, the reason is simple: the best present you can give your child is that they have fun on their birthday and that they not be put in a position of feeling in conflict about that fun. The collaborative rule for Dad in this situation is *adjust your agreements to fit your kid's needs.*

Is it legitimate to let your ex know that you're unhappy with the change of plans? Yes. Let her know, but do it in a calm voice, expressing your disappointment even as you acknowledge that plans change. You thus provide a model for your ex to perhaps reciprocate one day.

Be generous with your flexibility. If the kids want to be with their mom this year because all their cousins will be in town, although it's your turn for the holidays, don't make a big fuss about it. But also make it clear to your ex that you are not going to let this establish a precedent.

Be Proactive: What if the shoe is on the other foot? Say your mother wants to come to town for your child's birthday. If that's the case, give plenty of advance warning to everyone involved—maybe even the other Grandma. The collaborative father always keeps in mind that his new family arrangements require much more advanced warning than ever seemed necessary when he was still married and everyone was living under the same roof.

Ask for what you want, prepared with a plan for how it can be implemented. Consider your children's wishes, and incorporate those desires into your proposal.

Plan your holiday times well in advance. Two months' notice is not too much. One way to avoid disappointment is to communicate early and often with the children and your ex. If you do not communicate well in person, use email or even send a snail-mail letter. Give your children's mom plenty of time to think about your proposals and to respond. And keep in mind that pushiness usually produces more resistance than cooperation.

When making plans collaboratively, be specific. Take the time to have a conversation with the children's mom to decide which of you will have the kids on which days and for how long. Also make all transportation arrangements very clear as to times and who will be driving where.

Keep Your Agreements: This is a stressful time, especially for non-custodial parents. Try your best to hold yourself, your ex, and the kids to any agreements you make. Don't be a control freak about it. If you make a federal case of keeping agreements no matter what, you'll eventually just establish a reputation for being a jerk.

Include the Kids in Your Planning: Whenever it's reasonable, include your children in the planning. Let them help make the choices about when and where to celebrate the holidays, and with whom, but always make it clear that whatever you talk about has to be cleared with everybody involved. If you can't be with them on the special day, plan a time when you and the children can celebrate together. Be careful not to put a guilt trip on them about their desires for the holidays.

Create Two Holidays or Birthdays: Having two holiday or birthday celebrations for the children—one at your house, one at Mom's—is often a positive solution for extended families. Just make sure that the plans you make are collaborative and that they are made well in advance. This arrangement proves to the children that they have two homes and cements new family rituals and holiday customs. Don't worry about spoiling the children. More is better in this case, and they will be delighted with the double treat.

Be Nice: Especially during holidays, keep any bitterness you still feel over the divorce between you and your ex. If you can't say anything nice, just smile. Avoid putting the children in the awkward position of taking sides.

If You're Alone: Holiday time can trigger a resurgence of memories and melancholy feelings, especially if you are surrounded by happily married families. These difficult feelings can be magnified if you are not with the children. As holidays or birthdays approach, make special plans for the day. Visit with a friend or relative. Avoid being completely alone. Plan a short vacation with friends or do something special for yourself. Consider helping some less fortunate people if you cannot be with your loved ones. If there's an activity that you especially enjoy, be sure to spend time doing that, even if it costs a little more than you'd ordinarily spend on yourself.

Use Caution: I have a friend whose ex and he decided that in the spirit of being collaborative, they'd spend Christmas afternoon together, with the kids, just as in pre-divorce times. "How did it go?" I asked him a few days after the holiday. "Don't ask," he exclaimed. "It was miserable. Donna and I got into a major argument and things got nuts. I left the house two hours early with her screaming at me and both kids crying."

Even if things go pretty well, as they sometimes can, being together like this can be misleading for the children who might harbor hopes for your reconciliation. Most children have fantasies about that, with or without any encouragement from the parents. Be cautious and don't start something you don't know how to handle.

Build New Family Traditions: Divorced parents, especially dads, often make the mistake of trying to duplicate exactly what the family traditions were before the divorce. Create your own traditions for your new family, and let the children share in the planning. Take the opportunity to introduce traditions from your childhood, savoring the opportunity to share something with you own children that you enjoyed as a child.

Blended Families: If you remarry and your spouse has children, they will probably have their own ideas about how to celebrate holidays and birthdays. Discuss with your new partner ways that you can bring together the children from both sides of the family. Instead of imposing your own way of celebrating, get all the kids involved with planning what you'll do together. Ask questions and ask for suggestions from the kids. To encourage them to feel that they are more a part of the new routine, explore ways to include something from their own traditions. Maybe there are special foods or desserts that they associate with this or that holiday. Engage them in creating rather than imposing a totally new tradition.

Chill Out: Allow children to talk about the gifts they received and activities they engaged in with other family members they are visiting over the holidays. Children often feel that if they have a good time with one parent, it will hurt the other's feeling. Let them know they can show happiness with both parents.

Help your children shop for the other parent, sibling, grandparent, and/or stepparent. Children want to give gifts to the people in their lives just as adults do. Younger children have limited funds and often feel very awkward about buying gifts for the first few years after the divorce. Be kind. Make it easier on them by offering to take them shopping for "a present for Mom," their brother, or sister. If you are able to take a relaxed tone and be kind, they'll feel more comfortable being a part of both families.

Avoid the Indulgence Trip: Okay, one more time. Many divorced parents, especially dads, are still reeling from their personal hurt and guilt over the divorce. As a result, they may be overwhelmed by these feelings and respond to the children's pain by overcompensating with too much money or too many gifts. Perhaps the greatest lesson around doing things out of guilt is in the following statement by Audre Lorde: "I have no creative use for guilt, yours, or my own. Guilt is only another way of avoiding informed action, of buying time out of the pressing need to make clear choices, out of the approaching storm that can feed the earth as well as bend the trees."

If there is a single message to bring to your children during holidays and birthdays, it is a sense of things being okay, that, in spite of difficult times, there's still a space in our lives to celebrate our lives and who we are. This is ultimately the best gift, and perhaps the easiest one to give, though we may sometimes need to reach very deep within ourselves to find it.

CHAPTER TEN:

KIDS, FRIENDS, AND DATING

"When seeking your partner, if your intuition is a virtuous one, you will find him or her. If not, you'll keep finding the wrong person."
—*Joseph Campbell*

As a single father, issues around your love life are going to be a lot different than they were in your bachelor days. Some things are the same, but now you've got kids and an ex-wife; the challenge is going to be how you'll smoothly integrate your romantic life with being an accountable and loving parent. Since you are presumably continuing to pursue a collaborative relationship with your children's mother, you'll also have to be considerate of her and her feelings. These factors are unique to the lives of divorced fathers. Some say it takes between two and five years to dissolve the emotional bonds that once held you. Others claim it takes half the amount of time you were married. While that's not a hard-and-fast rule, one might err in the favor of caution and discretion in the interest of maintaining the collaborative spirit. And this caution and discretion are perhaps also the best way to move forward out of consideration for your children's emotions.

I'm not, of course, talking about allowing your fear of your ex-wife's—or your children's—reactions to your behavior to run your life. We are not responsible for each other's emotions. But it is possible to take responsibility for keeping your relationships as collaborative as possible. This won't happen if you're careless about bringing a new person into your life. After all, unless you're managing to keep the new person a total secret from your children and your friends for the long haul—not recommended—she will become a member of your family.

What exactly does all this mean in terms of developing a new relationship? To put it simply, it means stopping to consider how your ex and children are going to handle the news that you have a new love interest. If the letters I get from people through my website are any indication, most men have a tendency to rush into new relationships and to be pretty open about it, letting everyone in their lives know that they are *back in the game*. This is perhaps natural enough given the fact that the trials and tribulations you've undergone during these past months have kept you tied in knots. Whatever our motives, the potential fallout can be the same.

The most mature approach might be to sit down with your ex and openly share your feelings about dating. Is your ex going to be stung by the thought of you being with someone else? Would she like you to give her some warning that you are dating again?

Would she prefer to not have to face that for a few more months? How comfortable is she with the kids knowing that you are dating?

And what about you? Is seeing your ex with someone else going to set you off? Would it be a shock to you if you saw your ex's new lover doing a favor for her, such as repairing the plumbing in the house that had once been your home? Be as open yet diplomatic as you can be.

How will you approach the same topics with your children? If they are old enough, a conversation could be appropriate. Allow them to express their feelings, maybe even share their hopes that there could be a reconciliation between Mom and Dad. Listen, validate, and explain as compassionately as you can that you have the right to pursue happiness and love again.

When considering all this, it's easy to slip into a co-dependent trap of trying to take care of someone else's feelings or looking for ways to avoid an emotional blowout. At some point, your ex is just going to have to deal with the reality that you are no longer her husband and that you have a life of your own. Your kids will have to accept that there's no turning back, and there's good that can come from moving on.

As Kent related in his men's group, "Ah, the kids! All I can say is that hope springs eternal where they're concerned. Three years after the divorce and over a year into my new relationship with Gail, my kids are still asking when I'm coming home. Their mom and I are on pretty friendly terms and my shrink tells me that for better or for worse, this feeds the kids' hope that their mom and I will get back together. My oldest daughter, Tessa, tells me, 'Dad, you and Mom get along so good, I don't see why you can't get back together.' How do you explain stuff like that to a twelve-year-old girl? I just tell her that her mom and I decided that we are better as friends than we were as husband and wife and that's the way we've chosen to live our lives. Does Tessa buy it? Hell, I think she probably spends half her life turning it around in her mind, trying to understand what she can do to get her mom and me back together."

Because of your children's lingering hope, a new romantic partner for either parent is going to put them through some changes. It could anger the kids, and they might feel betrayed by the dating parent, worried that this new person might take you away from them, and scared that this could mean even more abandonment for them. What can you do about it? The key recommendation that family experts offer is to just keep reassuring your kids that you love them and always will, and that you will always be their dad.

But treat this time following the divorce as a transition period when you stay focused on making that transition as smooth and constructive as possible—for you, for your kids, and for your ex. Remember that freaking out your ex or angering your kids is going to create fallout for all of you and that will undermine any collaborative foundations you've gone to so much trouble to develop.

DATING BEFORE YOUR DIVORCE IS FINAL

Don't take romantic encounters lightly. Abstaining from dating until after your divorce is a strategic, emotional, and moral question. You've got to make your own decision around whether or not you, your kids, and your ex-to-be are emotionally ready to deal with bringing a new love into your lives.

In states where judges must consider fault in a divorce, they are primarily concerned about affairs they believe might have caused or contributed to the divorce. It's too difficult to attach a large amount of blame to an affair that began several months after legal separation. Just keep this in mind: In most states, the final leg of the divorce process involves settling all the legal and financial issues, so if your divorce has not been finalized, you would be wise to exercise restraint and keep your romantic endeavors tucked away.

Potential legal consequences aside, your priorities should be staying centered on maintaining the collaborative spirit and protecting your children. Maybe you'll be able to weather the storms of a divorce complicated by your dating, but if there is too much carryover of those storms into the years ahead, your efforts to foster a healthy extended family environment can get overly complicated. A well-managed collaborative divorce ultimately makes it possible to build a healthy, open, and collaborative extended family that can work together to make the lives of every member of that family a little less stressful and perhaps a lot easier.

READY OR NOT, BRING ON THIS NEW LIFE

If your divorce is final and all the papers are signed, the coast is relatively clear. At least on legal grounds, you now have an open path to begin a new romance. But before you do, take time to consider a number of issues that you probably didn't have to deal with ever before in your life. First and foremost is the idea that whoever you date seriously will, to one degree or another, become a member of your extended family, even if they never cross paths with your children, your ex, other family members, or close friends. Your new relationships can, and, in most cases will, have a direct or indirect impact on your family simply because they will have an impact on you.

Given that anyone you bring into your life can affect the whole family unit, it's more important than ever to heed the warning your mother probably offered you years ago—*don't rush into anything. Don't let well-meaning friends or relatives push you into dating prematurely.* Remember that this first relationship is where a great deal of healing can take place. And no matter how anxious you may be to jump into a new relationship, it's more important than ever to take stock of the collaborative values your new extended family will spur you to embrace.

As anyone who has ever been there will tell you, during those months immediately following your divorce, you are a man on the rebound, and it's difficult to know how long this will last. For some, it is just a few months. For others, it is years.

What exactly does it mean to be in this state? It primarily means that you're especially vulnerable. What's behind this vulnerability? It can be anything from your need to feel desirable and lovable again to the very dark side of seeking punishment for screwing up your marriage or looking for a way to get back at your ex for rejecting you. Depending on their intensity, these hidden motivations can be like magnets drawing you into relationships that you would normally avoid like the plague.

If you're still feeling pretty churned up emotionally, it may be better to concentrate on your inner needs, and building a solid and healthy relationship with your kids, than it is to plunge headlong into a new relationship. If you are constantly distracted by your feelings about the divorce—mourning the loss or celebrating it, caught up with anger, feeling betrayed or just plain disappointed—join a divorce group or find a good counselor or coach to work with. Reflect on conflicts you've had in past relationships, and try to learn what it was in you that got you stuck. Give yourself plenty of time to come to terms with your past so that you don't repeat it.

When you're truly ready to date again, it can be great for you and your kids. Intimate adult companionship is an important part of successful parenting. It allows you time to be a grown-up as well as a parent, to revitalize, and to explore the pleasure of a truly collaborative helpmate and friend.

While you might feel compelled to go out and quickly find a new mate to provide another parent for your kids, resist this urge. While it's nice if it happens, your kids are most likely better off with you alone than with your transitional or rebound romantic love interest. The nature of rebound romances is that they don't last. What will it mean to your children if they become attached to your new friend only to experience you breaking up with them? Don't forget—it could mean them going through the loss of a new friend, too. While children will most likely take that loss in stride, it is bound to have an impact on them, even if relatively small.

CHOOSE WISELY

Usually, we don't think too much about what attracts us to a person or what we really want in a relationship. What I've found in working with single fathers, however, is that the reality of being a dad tends to trigger some questions that might otherwise go unasked. No doubt, it's because we recognize that the choices we make at this point in our lives aren't quite as simple as they once were. What do men in our position look for in a new companion? The choices are as varied as the individuals making them, but here are some questions to ask:

- What specific qualities do you find attractive in a person? Physically? Emotionally? Intellectually? Spiritually? Personal motivations? Religious beliefs? Political beliefs?

- What specific qualities will complement you, your children, and your lifestyle? Are there activities and interests that you and your children enjoy that you'd like your companion to enjoy with you? How important is it that this person relates well to your kids? Is this a nurturing and patient person? How much or how little do they enjoy doing things for others?

- What type of companionship are you seeking: Do you want a friend? A date? Are you hoping to remarry? Sometimes, single fathers want to stay single, but have an adult in their lives with whom they can escape the pressures of family. Would this be you? Or are you looking for a person who can share your parental responsibilities and joys and with whom you might have another child?

- Are you willing to date another single parent? Chances are, if things work out well, this can lead to blending your families. Are you up for meeting the challenges of doing this? If you truly are, it can be a great adventure that benefits everyone. If you aren't up for it, it can be problematic, to say the least.

Now that you are older and hopefully wiser in the ways of the world, your chances for choosing and creating a successful love relationship will be better than it was first time around. But older doesn't necessarily mean wiser. Be cautious and intentional as you choose someone to welcome into your life and into the lives of your children.

You may discover, as you start to date again after your divorce, that you have doubts about your ability to maintain a long-term, loving relationship. This is natural enough and is experienced by most people in your position—especially after a second or third divorce! If you really screwed things up in your marriage, a little soul-searching is a good thing, but the point is not to get stuck in your emotional doubt and pain. You are not the same person today that you were a year or even a month ago. Let the past be in the past. We all learn our most important lessons from our mistakes. Do not let your past sense of guilt, blame, or shame interfere with your doing it right this time around. Just take an honest look, do your inner work, and move on.

If the fear of failure and rejection is so intense that it interferes with your ability to move on and find happiness, don't waste time. Get professional help. That's exactly what therapy, and occasionally medication, are designed for. Get over it and get on with it!

TELLING THE KIDS

I've mentioned this before, but I think that talking with your children about your decision to start dating is important enough to warrant further discussion.

When parents start dating, their children often aren't ecstatic about it. They may see this new person in your life—whom you are obviously very interested in—as competition for your affection. If they have fantasies about you and their mother getting back together, they may also attempt to protect that fantasy by ignoring or even being hostile toward your friend. Your dating might also reawaken their fears of abandonment, which they may have experienced when you and their mom first split up and you were no longer in their lives on an everyday basis. As one father put it, "My kids were just sure that anyone I even shook hands with was going to steal me away from them."

What can you do? You can be understanding and patient. Make it clear to your kids that you have friends just as they have friends. Make it clear to them that even though your friend sometimes spends a lot of time with you, she is not going to replace their mom. Tell them their mom will always be their mom and nothing will ever change that. Not now or ever. And you will always, always, always be their dad, no matter who else may come into your life. Reassuring them might take far longer than you would like, but suck it up and be patient. You might have to explain all this a hundred times, but eventually, your children will get it.

How do you judge whether or not a new relationship is significant enough to introduce to your family as a girlfriend? You'll know by the amount of time you are spending with her or because of your talking about your future together. You'll know because of the way you get along, and how well you can work out conflicts when they arise. And certainly, you'll know it if you are talking about getting married or living together.

Sometimes, when children, especially younger ones, see that you are relating to this new friend in an especially affectionate way, they might begin to allow themselves to open up emotionally and allow themselves to become positively involved with them. It would be a shame if they made this connection only to have you break it off with your friend. It happens; there's no doubt about it. It is just part of life. If you're on top of things as a parent, you'll then have to spend some time allowing your child to mourn that loss by simply sympathizing with them.

At the opposite end of the scale, some older kids are going to take the position that having a friend means that you're becoming a self-centered parent, more interested in dating than with healing conflicts in the family.

Keep in mind that if you bring a potential partner into your life and you spend a lot of time together with the kids, each child is going to have some reaction to that friend. If for no other reason, this is why it is best to know that the relationship you are entering into is serious and committed. My own recommendation is this: until you are pretty sure the new relationship is going somewhere, don't make your new friend a part of your home scene.

Okay, so you're quite sure you've found the new love of your life. You've tested the waters, she seems like she might just be the one, and you want to share your excitement and happiness with the kids. This is a big event for the kids, and there are no hard-and--fast rules for what to do or say.

How do you introduce them? In the end, it's not what you say so much as how you act toward your friend, the kids, and your former spouse during this time. The best advice I can offer is to stay on track with what you've learned about the collaborative way of life.

Children, even younger children, can be remarkably resilient, but it's important to keep in mind that there are limits to what they should be expected to handle. Whatever you do, don't avoid their questions or protests, and don't pull rank on them to end the fuss. Those tactics will only create further tension, and they are anything but collaborative. This is a time to call up all your resources for being understanding and compassionate toward your children, knowing these introductions can really bring up some fear and pain for them—and maybe for you! Let your kids know that you realize this makes them feel uncomfortable or how hard it is for them to think about bringing a new person into their life. Assure them that you will always be there for them, and you will always love them. Repeat this frequently.

If you have a child who is easy-going and who seems to openly accept your friend, they may or may not be showing their emotions. When my friend Ginger's ex-husband got remarried, they all thought everything was fine with four-year-old Grace. "Anything but!" Ginger told me. "Tom wanted her to be their flower girl. I was okay with that and thought Grace was, too. A week before the wedding, Gracie had a meltdown. I didn't see it coming. She broke out in a rash, and we thought she had the measles. The doctor said it was allergies, but we never discovered to what. When we got home from the doctor, Grace climbed into my lap and wept uncontrollably. I just held her and let her cry. When she finally stopped, she asked me, 'If Daddy marries Kate, where will you go, Mommy?' And that's when I got it. Poor little Grace! She thought if Tom married, Kate would become her mother and I'd disappear. I cry anytime I think of what a big load she was carrying. She actually thought Tom would send me away."

Grace had always been an easy-going, if not reticent child who rarely let others know her feelings. Everyone assumed that she was just a very flexible and laid-back kid. In fact, the incident involving Tom's wedding revealed to everyone that she was extremely sensitive and somewhat withdrawn into her own fantasies of how things worked in the world. Whenever potentially emotional issues arose after that, Ginger, Tom, and Kate always took extra time to give Grace plenty of opportunity to express herself.

This is an excellent example for me of not taking a child's reticence too lightly. Be careful, thoughtful, and considerate, as tender young souls want desperately for you to understand what they do not yet understand about themselves.

BE HONEST WITH THE OLDER KIDS

You can safely assume that your teenaged children will have a pretty sophisticated view of what's going on between you and your friend. This means that you're probably going to be okay talking with them openly. But don't assume too much. It's not just a question of how honest you can be with your teenagers; it's more a question of how much detail you should go into. With your older child, obviously, questions might go much deeper, and there might be more to what they're thinking and feeling than they are expressing.

Serena's mother Alee told her sixteen-year-old daughter about her father's new girlfriend. Serena immediately telephoned her father, Wayne. "I can't believe you didn't tell me first," Serena exclaimed. "Dad, I thought I was your closest confidante!"

Somewhat taken aback, but realizing his daughter was teasing him, Wayne came back with, "I was waiting for the right moment."

"Oh, get off it," Serena said. "You just chickened out, didn't you? You told Mom so she'd tell me."

While this wasn't exactly factual, it was true that he'd broached the subject first with Serena's mother, who had remarried the previous year, and asked her advice about how Serena should be told. When Alee volunteered to discuss it with Serena, he didn't protest.

"So, Pops," Serena said in a mocking tone. "Are you *getting it on* with her?"

Wayne, of course, was flabbergasted. "Hey," he said. "That's none of your business."

"Well, that probably means you are, doesn't it?" Serena said. "You're really embarrassed, aren't you?"

Wayne admitted he was. Only then did his daughter let up. "I'm sorry, Dad, I just had to give you a bad time. I'm actually really happy for you. I really am."

As Wayne would tell me later, "You never know quite what to expect from teenagers these days!"

Don't assume, however, that your teen with be as open and cheeky as Serena was. For a million different reasons, they could be quite uncomfortable with your having a serious girlfriend or knowing that you are getting married again. Take it one step at a time. Carefully listen to your son or daughter's responses—what they say, what their facial expressions tell you, if they show extra signs of stress, and what they body language says. Teenaged boys are usually practiced in deadpan responses, betraying little or no emotion. And the more emotional the situation, the flatter the deadpan expression. If you're simply getting nothing back—no words, no feedback of any kind—don't push it. Just put out a bit of information today, a bit more a few days from now, and so on. Chances are excellent that as they sit with this information, they will get curious about it and start asking questions. Be patient.

If you have two or more older children, talk with each one individually and tell them how you feel about this person. Give out only enough information at a time to test the waters. Be open. Tread lightly. Watch for the surfacing of different emotions. Be aware and sensitive to their responses, but don't let them run your life. You have every right to be happy, especially to have a happy, constructive, and loving relationship. In the long run, your fulfillment in this relationship can provide a positive model for them to see which will be a wonderful antidote to a contentious divorce between you and their mom.

IT'S NOT THE GIRLFRIEND VS. THE KIDS

When you're caught up in the pleasure and excitement of a new romance, you run the risk of unconsciously neglecting your children emotionally or even physically. It's important to keep spending quality time alone with your children a top priority even as this new relationship takes shape. If you're the non-custodial parent or if your children are with you for only brief periods of time, make sure that the kids get the majority of time with you. For example, your friend could come over for dinner one night. Or, especially if your time with the kids is limited, you can wait until the kids go back to your ex's place and then enjoy time with your girlfriend.

Both your children and your new friend are important to you, but don't let any of them completely run your life. You decide how to handle your choices, opportunities, and responsibilities. If your children don't like the person you date, or a person you date does not like your children, this will obviously not be a very workable way to live. Maybe they're jealous of one another, each wanting all of your attention and love. If you're feeling hassled or tense over this issue, talk with a professional counselor to help you sort through what is happening.

One of the big challenges in any relationship has to do with being clear what your own personal needs and wishes are. We all have to make some accommodations to the others we share our homes with. This can range from being careful not to leave your dirty socks on the living room floor to not dating other people. But there are core values and needs that are important enough to us, at a deeply personal level, that giving them up would mean abandoning ourselves for the sake of someone else's comfort.

What kinds of accommodations are going too far? What is non-negotiable? Your love for your children, for one thing. If they are truly important to you and your friend tells you that you must make a choice between her and them, you kiss your friend goodbye and never look back. And what if you love a certain kind of music and your friend hates it, and she asks you to never play it in the house? Well, that is probably going to be negotiable in most cases.

If you are going to live together in relative peace and have well-adjusted kids, you had better be able to respect each other's way of dealing with the daily contests that life lays at our feet—especially as it relates to your children. There's nothing wrong with expanding one's skills for dealing more effectively with life, but if your new someone is basically asking you to be other than who you are, it's usually a red flag telling you it's time to split.

While it's not always easy to find that thin line between demanding respect for who you are and accommodating the people you love, it's an important line to be aware of. Depending on how you handle that thin line, you'll provide your children with a model for either developing their own wholeness and inner strengths or becoming a slave to other's wishes and abandoning their greatest inner gifts.

WHEN YOUR EX STARTS DATING

So far, we've talked about your dating and how it impacts your kids and your ex. But what about when the shoe is on the other foot? How are you going to feel about your ex's dating? What's the collaborative principle to follow on this issue? It might be easier to say than to do: You can't control your former spouse's love life, but you can control your attitude toward her dating.

It is important to understand and accept the fact that you cannot choose whom or when your former partner dates. Even if you feel a great sense of relief to not be married to her anymore, you may be surprised to find waves of jealousy sweeping over you when you discover that she is involved with another person. This is normal. It's just part of going through a divorce. Let yourself be aware of these feelings. Share what you are feeling with a close friend. Long-standing relationships and feelings do not end or change the minute the judge signs the divorce decree. Yet, regardless of these feelings, do everything you can to take full responsibility for what you are feeling and don't lay them on your ex or your children.

How do we know when we're not holding these feelings responsibly? One sure sign is if we start making remarks to our children about "that bozo your mother is dating."

Count on it, when your former spouse begins dating or falls in love with someone else, it will stir up all sorts of feelings in you.

You may experience jealousy toward the new person, anger at be-ing replaced, sadness in realizing that the marriage is truly over, or fear that your children will like the new person more than they like you. Perhaps, you might even feel mingled happiness or relief that your ex is getting on with her life. It's going to take some time to deal with these feelings and fears. When that happens, take a deep breath, let it out slowly, then, be cool and polite, reminding yourself that the longer you hold onto old attachments to your ex, the longer it's going to take you to step fully into the new life you're creating for yourself and your kids.

Work every principle that you've learned about collaborative divorce, and you'll get through this one, too.

CHAPTER ELEVEN:

MARRYING AND BLENDING FAMILIES

"A good marriage is one which allows for change and growth
in the individuals and in the way they express their love."
—*Pearl S. Buck*

It's been said that a successful marriage is about sharing our lives with others, learning to be open, and being able to face difficult challenges together. But if feedback from others in men's groups and the online sharing is any indication, it is not so widely understood that second marriages, especially those where children are involved, have special challenges that first marriages don't have. This is particularly true for readers of this book since you have a child, or children, from your previous marriage and you have an ex-wife who is still involved in your life, however peripherally. Since she's the mother of your kids, you will have an ongoing relationship with her by virtue of the fact that you must, at the very least, coordinate visitation rights. If you've established a highly cooperative and friendly relationship with your ex-wife, it will be as if you have incorporated her into your extended family.

While this makes things more comfortable for the kids, and possibly for you, it may complicate your relationship with your new wife or partner. Consider it from your new spouse's point of view; she is not just dealing with a new relationship with you; she is also going to be dealing with your children and, hopefully to a lesser degree, your ex-wife.

Allow me to interrupt myself here with a reminder that the key to a healthy family system—especially a new, tentative family system—is the mutual love, caring, and respect that the spouses bring to that system. It's all too easy to forget in the midst of all the daily challenges and demands on us, that being alone together with your new spouse, as two mature adults who love each other, is essential. Take time to develop your bond, independent of the children and the daily parenting roles and family tasks. This is not a step that can be skipped! Getting away for a break may be difficult to arrange with all that's going on, but it is a key for building your own caring relationship, just the two of you, strengthening your ability to guide the new family. She will need your support and trust that, even though you have a continued relationship with the mother of your children, she's your partner.

Given those realities, it's good that you've been developing collaborative skills. They will be invaluable assets in your new relationship. With those tools and a down-to-earth overview of what marriage is all about, you'll be prepared to handle the issues that are inevitably going to arise, given the complexity of your life. Having a realistic picture of married life also helps. In that respect, if the joining of two people in marriage is comparable to blending two different cultures, then joining two people with past marriages and children must be comparable to blending two different planets. Not only are you marrying her, her children, and her family, but you are also inheriting her former spouse and his family. And, of course, she is marrying you and your children.

Don't forget the children's challenge; at this point, they most likely have two sets of parents and four sets of grandparents. This extended family inheritance, with all its attendant baggage, is going to take long-term, careful, and thoughtful integration and nurturing.

FALLOUT FROM THE KIDS

Children can be tolerant or even supportive of their parents re-marrying, but sometimes, they change their tune when real step-family life begins. Think about it this way: By the time you're ready for your next marriage, it might be a child's third family unit. The first was their biological parents' marriage (you and your ex); the second was the single-parent unit with you in one house, their mom in another; and the third would be the family unit being established with your new relationship. Each unit is a major adjustment for the kids. And each time, they had their own little worlds pretty much worked out. Now, with a stepparent coming in, the whole thing is starting over again. Another set of complicated routines to get used to. And . . . oops . . . who are these new step-siblings easing in on our life?

We've noted elsewhere that it's quite normal for kids to hold on to the hope that Mom and Dad will get back together and life will return to how it once was—even if how it once was wasn't a particularly happy scene. Healing from family split-ups isn't easy. Allow the kids space to mourn yet another change in their world, even if you think that it's ultimately a change for the better.

In most cases, emotional and spiritual healing from divorce takes time; in fact, the average person requires two or more years before they can actually be discerning about a new relationship. But in the midst of your own adjustment to these changes, don't lose touch with what the kids are going through. Pay attention to their grieving process because most often, they are not mature enough to explain why they are unhappy. Instead, their discontent usually shows up in negative actions and attitudes, particularly toward those they might view as *interlopers* in their lives—and that can most certainly mean the new love of your life and her children.

Be ready for the possibility of a new round of challenges and negative acting out from your kids as well as hers as your two families begin to merge and blend. It's not unusual for children to act out, either positively or negatively, in an effort to establish their position in the power structure of the new family culture. Try to allow a great amount of time and lots of forgiveness so children will have an opportunity to feel at ease in the new extended family. Don't take every mischievous behavior too seriously.

"For months after our two families came together," Jonathan told me, "Leela, Willa's six-year-old daughter, clung to her mom like glue. My daughters, who were ten and twelve at the time, certainly reached out to Leela, but not with much luck. Slowly, what came out was Leela's fear of losing her mom. Seeing her mother find what she called 'a new daddy,' was bad enough for her. Seeing that this new daddy came with two new females was an added threat in her mind. I didn't understand it, and neither did Willa. But as we just dealt with it, what came out was that when Leela's father had an affair, he rejected both Willa and Leela, and her father's lover had actually treated this little girl with uncensored hostility. Leela somehow saw my daughters as being like her father's lover and was afraid of being rejected all over again. In time, she gained confidence in all of us and, as far as I can tell, her wounds are healed."

Time, patience, open communication, and active listening are the only ways to get to the root of a child's uncertainty. Your attention will obviously be divided, but make an effort to see the struggles and give individual love and care.

FALLOUT FROM YOUR EX

Hopefully by the time you are ready to remarry, you will have buried the hatchet with your former spouse and ended the domestic wars between you. With a little help from your friends, maybe the two of you are relating well enough that you would consider inviting her to your wedding. May it be so! But be prepared for a new round of stressful thoughts and tender feelings rising to the surface because your new marriage will finally send the signal to all concerned that you and your ex are not getting back together.

While it can be good for the children from your previous relationship to see their mother supportive of your new relationship, don't expect it to be without some strife. Emotions can range from anger, rage, and depression, to non-cooperation, withdrawal, and/ or conscious sabotage. This is the time to be mindful and considerate about your own and your former spouse's feelings; after all, this is the person who once loved you and who you once loved, and is still connected to you as family through the children. She may be like a second cousin to you now, but she can't be totally ignored, either.

But what if it's your former wife getting remarried, and you're not? While there might be a tendency to act like a jerk, this is definitely another opportunity for you to become a grown-up and deal with life's tough transitions in a graceful manner. It might be that you haven't gotten over her yet and you still fantasize about getting back together. On the other hand, maybe you're ecstatic that someone is finally hooking up with her because she still calls you every time something needs to be fixed in the house. Whether you feel relieved or you are wondering why you are in grief, your ex getting married is bound to put you through some emotional changes, big or small.

Take a deep breath. Think about the kids, and don't do anything that will make them embarrassed or make you ashamed or humiliated. While you don't have to be enthusiastic about your ex's marriage, you do need to be civil and not abandon your fatherly role as a strong and compassionate family leader. You might be unhappy and pissed off, but that doesn't give you the license to be a jerk.

One of the letters sent to my website presented the following problem: "My ex married a total *a-hole* and frankly I didn't want the guy within a mile of my kids. They invited me to their wedding, but I didn't go. Over the past few months, Dale has left a dozen messages on my voice mail, wanting to get together with me. He says it's for the kids. The only thing I think would be good for the kids is if Dale got lost. Maybe I'm off the wall on this but I don't think so. What's other people's experiences with this kind of thing?"

Several other men sent in notes about their experiences, most of them recommending that the above letter-writer agree to a meeting with the new spouse and find out what was going on. The best answer sent in was the following:

"Sounds like you're pre-judging Dale. Maybe he's an *a-hole* like you say, but I'm suggesting you could also be the bigger one here. Look, the guy is making an effort to bridge the canyon between you and him for the sake of your kid. I'd suggest getting off your high and mighty horse, and at least giving this guy a chance.

"This advice comes from being in a similar place as you. I'm not trying to tell you what to do. I didn't speak to my ex or her old man for over a year after they got married. I got over myself when I saw my son and his stepdad getting along fine. In fact, since then, his stepdad and I have become pretty good friends. He has two kids by a prior marriage, too, which makes me think we're all in this together, and I'm not the only one who has ever gone through a divorce. Last summer, I helped him build a playhouse at his ex's house, if you can believe that. It's been quite a journey. So, I say, lighten up and find out what's happening with this guy. There might be some good surprises in store for you and everybody involved."

DO WE REALLY HAVE TO TALK ABOUT THIS?

While you are making plans for your second marriage, the subject of prenuptial agreements just might come up, initiated either by you or your prospective new spouse. If you've been through a nasty divorce, with battles over money and property, and have recovered financially, you might be particularly sensitive to this issue. For example, you might want to feel secure that a certain portion of your estate go to your children when you die. If you are involved in a family business, you might want to make certain that your interests as well as the other family members' interests are protected should the unspeakable happen. If you are going to become a full-time, stay-at-home parent, you will want to discuss how you and your spouse-to-be view the meaning of equality. And if your fiancée or you have contracts, debts, or have gone through bankruptcy recently, you may want to do something to keep those debts and financial responsibilities separate.

Why bring up money in a chapter dealing with love and the emotional issues surrounding a second marriage? It's because money problems between husband and wife can quickly turn into emotional problems. In fact, discussions around money will reveal a lot to you and your fiancée about how you both view equal partnership in a marriage.

The best way to open such a discussion is not by introducing it as a prenuptial issue but as a discussion about values you both hold around what it means to have a true partnership. In the process, you'll hopefully learn what kind of financial foundation you are starting out with.

Initiating a discussion about a prenup isn't necessarily easy or comfortable. When we're in love, we don't want to talk about money, and certainly not about a possible divorce. And yet, taking the time to sit down and discuss your views of who owns what and what you and your fiancée view as equality in marriage can be one of the most important discussions you'll have.

Find out all you can about drawing up a prenuptial agreement before you sit down together for such a discussion. Then, choose a time when you are both relaxed to discuss it, starting out by saying something like, "I'd really like us to sit down and talk about our future together, the lifestyles we find comfortable, as well as how we each handle our finances. I want to share some things like this with you now so it won't be hanging over our heads when we get married."

Don't let a discussion about prenups fall to the bottom of your priority list just because you are uncomfortable talking about it. If there are details that are potentially problematic, it is much better to talk about them now rather than later. If you can't come to an agreement now, imagine what it could be like six months or a year from now when you discover that the savings you pooled into your joint savings account is going to your new spouse's ex-husband who wanted a little extra help because he needed to have his car repaired.

BLENDING THE OLD AND THE NEW

Blended families should come with a warning: "Fragile: Handle with Care." At first, everyone involved—your children, her children, each of you—might have difficulty coping with the enormous changes that are thrust upon him or her as they work out the logistics of the new living arrangements. Who gets which room? Who gets to choose the breakfast food when you go shopping? You and your new spouse might begin to feel like referees at the World Wrestling night on big screen TV. Getting through this can require negotiating skills, a great deal of patience, and the ability to have a great deal of compassion for other people's wounds and broken hearts.

The one thing you'll need a lot of is the ability to look beyond the surface behaviors and understand how to help broken hearts mend. Holding family meetings, seeking occasional outside counsel, or joining a stepfamily support group are your options. Don't despair, because time, love, understanding, and acceptance of each other's feelings and sensitivities will likely heal these issues and build some strong bonds that can last a lifetime. Be gentle and make plenty of room for the blending to take place.

You can eliminate a great amount of stress in the blending process, and head off many potential disasters, by making sure that each member feels loved and wanted. Husbands and wives set the standards of behavior and caring by showing a deep love and respect for one another. Since it's way too easy for a quiet family member to fall between the cracks and feel unwanted, you must make conscious and heart-centered choices to love all members equally, even if they really bug you. Make time for the individual. Love in the blended home begins with the mom and dad and spreads to embrace the children.

You'll probably discover that the greatest challenge of remarrying comes about because your new wife is entering an already established system. That system evolved with the presence of a person (your ex-wife) that your new wife may or may not have met. How are you going to help her adjust to this system and how is that system going to embrace her? The odds are that the children are going to test you to see if she is truly *good enough* to earn membership in this system, though they'll do it in a very personal and usually confrontational way. Your responsibility is to work closely with her and to take part in building a sense of security, safety, and happiness for all concerned.

This challenge obviously is heightened and further complicated if she comes with children and an ex of her own. There are now two systems established with different, competing variables.

Understand that you and your new partner need to be the ones guiding your children; and you all want to end up at the same destination, teaching values that are respectful of every family member. This is a discussion to have before remarriage, but certainly a reality every day afterward.

Very often, we have fantasies of creating a perfect family union. You as well as your new spouse may be expecting everyone to have unconditional love for everyone else. You love your new wife's children, and she loves yours. But the chances are that if you and your new wife have only been together a few months, you probably don't even know the kids very well. Maybe everyone has been on his or her best behavior. Or maybe they've been little brats. Either way, you need to take the position that you are entering unknown territory—both you and your new spouse. Tread softly. And give it time.

The issue of disciplining the children is particularly problematic because you cannot be very effective in that role until the child has learned who you are and has established some kind of a bond with you. Until then, disciplining needs to be the responsibility of the biological parent, but with agreement with you (the stepparent) about goals and expectations. There may be disagreements between you and your new partner about these matters, so take the time to sit down and discuss them on a regular basis. If you are expecting everything to be done your way, forget it. The most successful blended families are the result of a lot of compromise and a lot of skillful communication.

Respect one another and let the relationships build on their own merit, without undue pressure to fulfill the fantasy of everybody loving one another from day one.

NEW FAMILY, NEW RITUALS

Just as it's important to blend the aspects of the old family systems to provide consistency and security, it's important for new families to develop their own rituals. As your new family comes together, pay close attention to everyone's needs and expectations. Take time to learn about other members of your new family—what their needs are, what their fears are, how flexible or inflexible they are in their dealings with you and other family members—and create new traditions to accommodate the different needs.

As you are getting to know each other, be open in your communications. If the children are old enough to participate in family meetings and discussions, be sure to include them and invite them to participate at whatever level is appropriate, given their ages. This will help to give all members a sense of belonging to a new intimate group.

Whatever rituals and customs you bring in will, if appropriate, become part of your new family culture, but new holiday rituals should be developed that are unique to the present constellation. For example, an Episcopalian woman marries a Jewish man, and so Chanukah celebrations might be added to Christmas; the children learn new rituals and expand their philosophies for living. Other elements, such as specific kinds of jokes or well-intentioned family goofing and humor can also go a long way toward weaving a family together. Humor and playtime can be a divine bonding experience. Finding ways to laugh together—like weekly game nights or taking turns sharing a joke at the dinner table—will go a long way toward establishing a sense of belonging to each other.

SIBLING RIVALRIES

Feuds between step-siblings can form patterns of behavior that are repeated again and again throughout a person's life. Classic sibling rivalry occurs when a child feels he or she must compete with a brother or sister for their mother or father's attention. This can be magnified when there is a blended family, since the child can feel that there are just too many people competing for Dad's attention. Rivalries can develop not just because the child feels there is too much competition, but also because one or both parents simply haven't been emotionally available to anyone. Kids shouldn't be expected to have great insights about that; after all, adults don't always see it. Rest assured, however, that when Dad's not available emotionally, each child is going to have the feeling that he or she is the only one not getting the love and attention they want. And what most kids will experience is that he or she feels deprived because all the love is being given away to someone else. If you are blending families with kids on both sides, it's easy for every kid to blame this on a sibling. Actually, it can start when you are still dating and have introduced your kids with hers. And it can rise all over again if you have a new baby together.

The best-case scenario of bonding with stepmom and developing friendships with new step-siblings doesn't come automatically. If you see conflicts developing early on, first recognize that they are normal under the circumstances, and then accept the fact that if you're going to successfully blend your lives, you might need the help of a family counselor. If you get a head start on sibling rivalries, recognizing what to expect, and learn how to handle early conflicts, you've got a good chance of making your expanded family work really well.

One of the great challenges for a youngster, particularly one who's been an only child for a number of years, is having a new baby come into the house. The insecurity and jealousy which bubbles up at such a time is a completely natural phenomenon, and you can't really stop it from happening. However, there are a few tips to help you keep it from getting out of balance. Yes, you might need to take corrective action, but always keep in mind that it's really hard on a kid to lose the favored place as the baby of the family. Cut the kid a little slack, and assure the older child that you love them. In many cases, getting the older child to participate in getting ready for the baby can help them feel that they are important and are contributing to this new change.

As your new wife begins to show her pregnancy, get some books that are age-appropriate for the older child that help to explain what's going as the baby grows in its mother's body. (Yes, this is for boys, too!) Most children will become increasingly curious and interested in the birth. Have them help you fix up the new baby's room. Ask them to help you pick out equipment you'll need. The more involvement the child can experience, the better. He or she needs to feel included in the planning and preparations, and the more they feel included, the less trouble with rivalry you'll be likely to see.

All the changes you and your new partner are creating in your lives take time to bring to full fruition. Be patient. Don't get down on yourself or any of your other family members if what you envision doesn't happen all at once. Creating a healthy family is a true collaborative effort, one that works best when you include the youngest as well as the oldest in any and all major decisions. All the collaborative experience you accumulated while dissolving your previous relationship now comes full circle, for these are life skills that apply to all human challenges, now carrying you toward one of life's greatest rewards—the creation of a relationship to endure the test of time.

BASIC RULES OF COLLABORATIVE DIVORCE

- **Remember to Be Nice:** Try hard to be nice and polite. Mutual respect goes a long way toward creating peace.

- **Establish the 24-Hour Rule:** Insist on twenty-four hours to think over any significant decision you're faced with.

- **Spare the Kids:** Train yourself to never complain to the kids about their mom. They should never have to make choices about their loyalties to you or your ex.

- **Don't Burden the Kids with Your Pain:** Never release your anger or frustration on the kids. From the children's point of view, they need the love of both parents.

- **Third-Party Help:** Recognize when you are stuck and seek professional help when you are.

- **Create Clear Boundaries:** Draw clear lines about how you want to be treated and accept nothing less than that.

- **Ask for What You Want:** Rather than being defensive or making her guess what you really want, practice saying and asking for exactly what you want. After putting out your requests, ask her to take twenty-four hours to get back to you with an answer.

- **Let Her Have Her Way While Not Giving Up Yours:** Search for ways that both of your needs or wishes can be satisfied. Sometimes this is possible by finding an alternative way of looking at the problem you seem to be stuck on.

- **Listen to Her Complaints without Defending Yourself:** Learn to be a proactive listener. Even if she is complaining about you, listen without defending yourself, remembering that you do not have to agree with her view of you. Then, give yourself time to consider your response.

- **Find Ways to Agree:** Find things to agree on and constantly remind each other about these.

- **Switchover Day Stress:** It isn't easy for kids to switch back and forth between your home and their mom's. Yes, you'll be called "Mom" instead of "Dad" sometimes. And the kids will forget whose house rules they're supposed to follow. Be patient. And keep your sense of humor.

- **Establish Ground Rules for Meetings:** Meetings can be explosive, especially in the early days when tensions are high. When you must sit down to talk over difficult issues, go in with a clear agenda. Agree on special antidotes when tempers flare—leave the room to calm down, write out your thoughts, etc.

- **Make Peace, Not War:** Forget about proving who's right, who's wrong, and who betrayed whom. Put your kids first. You can't fix the past but you can make the present and future better.

ACKNOWLEDGMENTS

Many fathers, mothers, children, therapists and doctors, lawyers, and clergy have contributed their stories of struggle, transformation, and hard-won understanding to this book. While they remain unnamed, to all of them I'm truly grateful.

My appreciation to Hal Zina Bennett, my writing guru, for making this book come alive with wit, wisdom, and clarity.

Thanks to Lindsay Sandberg, my editor at Familius, whose devoted and elegant editorial skills made this a lively and easy-to-follow book.

To Judy, my wife and love of my life, my words fall short describing how much your encouragement, support, and belief in me made this meaningful project come to fruition.

ABOUT THE AUTHOR

PAUL MANDELSTEIN founded the Father Resource Network to provide coaching and support services to help men meet the challenges of fatherhood today. Paul is a pioneer in the field of personal communications technologies and body/mind/spirit publishing; as president and publisher of The Book Publishing Company, he directed a line of books in the family planning, comparative religion, and community lifestyle categories. Along with other milestones in publishing, he published the first *Dummy's Guide*, selling millions of copies and kicking off that genre. Paul is also the author of *The Nightingale and the Wind* and *Queen Emmali and the Enchanted Lute*, both illustrated new mythology folktales focused on gender equality, freedom, and empowerment. Paul is a divorced father with four children and four grandchildren.

ABOUT FAMILIUS

Visit Our Website: www.familius.com

Familius is a global trade publishing company that publishes books and other content to help families be happy. We believe that the family is the fundamental unit of society and that happy families are the foundation of a happy life. We recognize that every family looks different, and we passionately believe in helping all families find greater joy. To that end, we publish books for children and adults that invite families to live the Familius Nine Habits of Happy Family Life: *love together, play together, learn together, work together, talk together, heal together, read together, eat together,* and *laugh together.* Founded in 2012, Familius is located in Sanger, California.

Connect

Facebook: www.facebook.com/paterfamilius

Twitter: @familiustalk, @paterfamilius1

Pinterest: www.pinterest.com/familius

Instagram: @familiustalk

FAMILIUS

The most important work you ever do will be within the walls of your own home.